NEVER DRINK CALORIES

Theories of an Anorexic

never drink calories

theories of an anorexic

jennifer otto

Mill City Press
Minneapolis, MN

Mill City Press, Inc.

212 3rd Avenue North, Suite 290

Minneapolis, MN 55401

612.455.2294

www.millcitypublishing.com

ISBN-13: 978-1-936400-59-1

LCCN: 2010940649

Cover Design by Alan Pranke

Typeset by Sophie Chi

Printed in the United States of America

table of contents

in memory of angela

And now I try hard to make it
I just want to make you proud
I'm never gonna be good enough for you
I can't pretend that I'm alright
And you can't change me
'Cuz we lost it all
Nothing lasts forever
I'm sorry, I can't be perfect

–Simple Plan, "Perfect"

preface

Between 4 and 20 percent of young women practice unhealthy patterns of dieting, purging, and binge-eating; 78 percent of eighteen-year-old girls are unhappy with their bodies. Why, you might ask? Pressure. Pressure to be thin. Pressure to have a perfectly proportioned body. Pressure to eat socially acceptable amounts of food when in public. Pressure to be perfect. But how is that even possible? How can anyone be perfect when there is no such thing?

We all strive to be the "ideal" person…the ideal spouse, the ideal parent, the ideal friend, the ideal lover. But why can't we just accept who we are? The truth is, most of us are too concerned with what "he" is thinking and what "she" is saying to even concentrate on who we really want to be. This has to change.

It finally changed for me after years of painful isolation, starvation, and self-mutilation. I learned how to accept myself and to be proud of who I am. By surviving multiple life-threatening events, I was able to struggle past the insecurities that life perpetuates and realize that the purpose of life wasn't just about pleasing others. It was about pleasing me.

But as I mentioned, it took me years to reach this point of self-acceptance. I had been motivated to please others my entire life. As a shy child, I never shared any of my feelings with any adults and rarely to my peers. The fear of being laughed at haunted my existence. I never wanted to start trouble, so I always kept a smile on my face and my opinions to myself. I remained agreeable in order to be socially acceptable.

I grew up in a small New Jersey suburb, about forty-five minutes outside of New York City, with both parents and a younger sister. My mother, a strong, selfless perpetual worrier, had been raised on a farm out in western Pennsylvania and had lived an extremely sheltered life. It seemed as though her sole purpose during my childhood was to give me all that she didn't have as a child. Meanwhile, my father was just the opposite. Distant and insensitive, he was raised in a New Jersey upper-class neighborhood with all he could ever want or need. This combination constantly left me pushing my mother away while fiercely attempting to gain my father's attention.

Aside from my parents' incoherent relationship with me, they were disjointed from each other as well. Throughout my childhood, I could certainly sense a vast distance between them. Although we went on family vacations together and spent weekends barbequing with our neighbors, the family dynamic was definitely off. As I grew older, I realized my parents never spent any time together alone, which seemed a bit strange. They were hardly even in the same room together. My dad would glue himself to the TV in the basement while my mom would use the living room to read. Our family dynamic certainly wasn't the norm compared to my friends' families, but it had become normal for us.

Separate from each other, my parents were great parents. My father took my sister and me to baseball games and on rafting trips. He taught us how to fish and the words to every

Billy Joel song ever composed. My mom did everything for us from taking us to our after-school activities to being class mother and making Halloween costumes. Both of them fully supported me in everything I did. They always praised my good grades but never pressured me to achieve all A's. All they asked was that I tried my hardest, but my own perfectionist tendencies didn't allow me to settle for mediocrity. I always strove to be the best.

With all of my talents, good grades, and activities, I was still missing something. I got enough attention from my family. I had supportive parents who loved me very much. I had great friends. What more did I need? Well, I needed to stand out in some way. I needed to feel like I was special. And I found my special talent by starving myself...starving myself for seven long years. And for what? To learn what I should have already known, what teachers and parents tell us throughout our entire lives. We are all special, just by being ourselves.

Unfortunately, I learned this lesson the hard way. I developed an eating disorder, a journey into an endless, what I thought to be hopeless, seven-year battle with complete isolation, obsession, and depression. Fasting, purging, bingeing, cutting, overdosing—whatever means of self-mutilation I could think of to make me feel special and stand out from everyone else. I cannot infer just one cause for my disorder. Disordered eating is caused by a combination of social pressures, psychological issues, and family dynamics. This is what makes eating disorders so complex and difficult to treat. It takes a lot of time and commitment to overcome.

I wanted to share my experience with the rest of the world with hope of helping those who are suffering from eating disorders by giving them inspiration. I also aspire to teach those who want to help their loved one through the recovery process. I want to educate the world with my understanding of eating disorders. I want to help explain what is going on in one's mind when suffering from an eating disorder so those who may not suffer from one can gain better insight. Reading about my recovery will hopefully inspire those struggling to reach out to those who love them and support them and to get help.

Most often, those who suffer from eating disorders want help, but they are scared of getting better. They are scared of losing the control they think they have. They are scared of losing their "identity," but the funny thing is, they are essentially hiding it. Getting help allows one to show their true colors and unmask their true selves from this terribly controlling disease. Recovering means regaining control over your life instead of letting the eating disorder control you.

To those suffering, my story will bring you into my mind and show you that I was exactly like you. I thought the same thoughts as you. I rationalized things exactly the way you do. But I also did the unthinkable. I recovered 110 percent. I can show you that anyone can recover from an eating disorder, because I did.

You can buy your hair if it won't grow
You can fix your nose if he says so
You can buy all the makeup that MAC can make
But if you can't look inside you
Find out who am I too
Be in a position to make me feel so damn unpretty

– TLC, "Unpretty"

1 | how it all began

It was Labor Day weekend, 1990, the weekend before I entered the seventh grade. My mom decided she would take my friend Melissa, my sister Meredith, and me to the Jersey Shore for the weekend. Excited for the beach, I quickly packed a few pairs of shorts, a bunch of tee shirts, and two designer bathing suits including my favorite rainbow-colored leopard-printed one-piece. For reading material, I crammed a new book called "Your Fourteen-Day Shape Up Plan" into my beach bag. I had just received this book from the school mail-order program two days before leaving for the beach. It taught me many new concepts: how to count calories, how to calculate how much I should weigh depending on my height, and how to tone each "target area." It even included a chart of common foods and their fat content.

The first night there, I sat in our musty wood-paneled motel room on one of the tiny full-sized beds skimming through the third chapter of my new book. After I paged through each exercise, I would routinely flip back to the cover to view the beautiful, curvaceous girl draped with a clingy purple-striped leotard and nude tights, fashionably finished off with baby pink legwarmers. Each time I glanced at the cover, my eyes would focus on her perfectly proportioned body, toying with the idea that if I did everything this book told me to do I could have her thighs, her stomach, and her legs. I could have the perfect body just like she did.

I immediately laid down on my side on top of the hideous brown cigarette-stained comforter, with the exercise directions in view, and got to work. With a little bit of coaxing, I convinced my friend Melissa to join me. Of course, I thought this was a harmless act—two young girls taking time out of their day to tone their problem areas. I knew at that time that I wanted to make this a routine, but I never imagined that it would turn into a vital obsession.

The next day at the beach was absolutely wonderful. I felt nice and slim in my one-piece bathing suit with my 5’6”, 115-pound frame. Melissa and I sprawled out on our towels, on top of the dry hot sand, chatting about the cute boys in our grade. Throughout our conversation, I couldn’t help but notice the different women walking by. Some were bigger than me, and some were smaller. At one point, an extremely muscular brunette wearing a yellow bikini strutted by us. She seemed so self-confident. Self-assured. That’s what I wanted. If I could have her body, I knew I would have the extra confidence that I needed.

In order to do so, my immediate goals were to cut down on calories and increase my exercise. We returned to our hotel room after the beach for a quick snack before dinner. I grabbed a bag of sour cream and onion potato chips, one of my favorites, and for the first time, I read the nutritional information on the back. I needed to learn the calories per serving. That afternoon I ate exactly thirteen chips for a total of 150 calories. As much as I wanted that fourteenth chip, my willpower would not allow it.

From that moment forward, my dieting and exercising became routine. During the first year of my newfound hobby,

I didn't drop a lot of weight—maybe just a few pounds—but the mental obsession became strong. I was always aware of what I ate and how much I exercised. I had accomplished the control that others sought. I bragged about it, too, in order to get the attention I so desired. Attention was the main thing I was trying to achieve. For some reason, I just didn't feel like I got enough of it.

In early February, my friend Rachel hosted her thirteenth birthday party at her house. It was a typical middle school party, including movies, food, and games. At some point during the festivities, my mind drifted, as it normally would in these types of social situations. Nothing particular came to mind, just that I was bored and felt that no one was paying any attention to me. I was overwhelmed. I needed to be alone and away from the crowd. I decided to go hide in the closet, partly just to see if anyone would notice. I sat for hours, at first trying to nap and then eventually thinking about why they hadn't noticed me missing. Did they even notice my existence, or could I be dead and no one would care? I finally heard faint voices asking about my whereabouts, and then they began their search. They finally found me but thought nothing of my disappearance. They thought it was a funny joke, assuming I had been gone for only a short while. If only they had known it was a cry for help. If Rachel's mother knew how long I'd been gone and understood that it was because I was depressed, I'm sure she would have said something to me and to my mother, but nothing was said. Everyone just laughed about it, like I was playing a good old game of hide-and-seek. Although it was only for a brief moment, I was somewhat satisfied, as I had received some attention. However, I still craved more.

For the first day of eighth grade, I convinced my mother to let me wear a new black button-down collared shirt with lime green, cherry red, and deep purple patches sewn on the front; the bottom half of the shirt was made out of a sheer material, which allowed my flat stomach to peek through. I felt slim that day yet still self-conscious due to my hideous metal braces and mid-length bangs that I was desperately trying to grow out. At fourteen years old, I was taking ballet lessons four nights a week, sometimes two classes a night. I was eating very little, but I was still eating.

I came home from my first day of school and poured myself a large glass of Diet Coke with ice in one of my Snoopy glasses I had collected from McDonalds. My mom spent the entire evening with me, helping me cover all of my new books with paper garbage bags and buying new notebooks, pencils, and erasable pens at the local CVS Pharmacy. By eight p.m., I made sure I was in my pajamas and ready to watch my favorite show, *Full House*. "Meredith, can't you go and finish that in the kitchen?" I asked with an annoyed tone. My sister was eating ice cream and she always chewed with her mouth open. It made it difficult to hear the TV and, more importantly, it also made it tempting to get a bowl for myself. Instead of leaving the room, Meredith gave me a nasty look and continued to eat her cookie dough ice cream. I rolled my eyes and forced myself to focus back on the TV. I didn't want to miss a thing.

The episode began by focusing on my favorite character, DJ, a fourteen-year-old eldest sister of three. The premise was simple. She had been invited to a swimming party and decided she was too fat to wear a bathing suit to the event. Therefore, she proceeded to put herself on a two-week starvation diet in order to lose weight. For inspiration, she taped magazine cutouts of skinny girls all over the refrigerator. Additionally, she worked out obsessively at the gym and threw out her brown-bag lunches every day before she left for school. Her mission was simply to exercise as much as possible while eating as little as possible.

Of course, DJ fainted before the episode ended, proving to her audience that extreme dieting was not a healthy solution. The half-hour television show finished with DJ and her father having a serious heart-to-heart and sharing a giant hug. The morale of the story should have been straightforward. However, I interpreted the message in my own convoluted way. By the following Monday, I had magazine cut-outs of girls in swimsuits posted on my wall and was throwing out my sandwiches at school. I was determined to lose weight.

Months passed by and I finally began gaining attention for my actions. Proud of my incessant willpower, I vocalized my habits, especially the fact that I was only drinking water for lunch on a daily basis. By springtime, I had lost too much weight and my friends started to become worrisome instead of envious. Many of my friends didn't know what eating disorders were, so they thought they could just make me eat.

One day during lunch, my friends and I were outside sitting on the picnic tables in the courtyard. I was just drinking water, as usual. My friend Jamie insisted that I eat something. I made a big fuss, in order to ensure everyone could hear I was refusing. She even tried stuffing a pretzel in my mouth in front of all our friends. I spit it out into my hands and threw it away. She then proceeded to tell me that if I didn't eat anything she would never talk to me again. She also told everyone not to talk to me until I ate. But I told her and everyone else that if they didn't talk to me, I would starve myself even more. What control I had. The attention I was getting was inconceivable. So I continued my extreme dieting and the hard work soon paid off.

By spring, I had lost ten pounds and was down to 105. The first to notice was my ballet teacher. During a Monday night master technique class, she warmly praised me for my weight loss. "Jen, have you been losing weight? Oh my gosh! You are almost as skinny as Erin (an eighty-pound classmate who was naturally small-boned). I can't believe it! I'm so jealous."

Well, those were the three little words I was subconsciously waiting for: *I'm so jealous.* It was incredibly satisfying to have someone jealous of me. I mean, who am I? What makes me so special? Why would anyone be jealous of me? Now I had the control that other women envied. Not to mention a ridiculously skinny body. What more could I want?

Unfortunately, going to dance class had now become a stressful event since I was more conscientious of my body, especially in a leotard. Although I had lost weight, my body image had started to become distorted, so I felt that I was much larger than I actually was. In my mind, I suspected my classmates thought I was a blimp. Looking around the room during each class, I compared each and every body part to mine. "Well, her butt is smaller than mine, and her legs are skinnier than mine. Her wrists are smaller than mine. Just a few more pounds, just a few more," I thought to myself. I knew I could look as skinny as those girls. Just a few more pounds and I'd be all set.

In addition to wanting to look good, I also thought that being skinnier would make me a better dancer. At this point, I felt that everyone else was better than me. I felt that everyone could just look at me and feel better about themselves. In my mind, everyone could turn better than I could. They could all leap higher than I could. Their upper body movement was cleaner than mine. Their arches were nicer than mine. The list went on and on and on.

However, losing those ten pounds was helping me realize there was one thing that I was better at: losing weight. All of the other girls loved food. They would talk about it nonstop. They'd brag about their scrumptious burger from McDonald's or the delicious Oreo cheesecake their mom made the night before. You see, I was already one step ahead of these girls. What were they thinking? They had absolutely no self-control. I, on the other hand, had all the control in the world.

I could easily control what went into my mouth and what didn't and I was very proud of that talent. It felt so good to not eat. I felt such a sense of accomplishment, something that these other girls would never be able to feel because they had to eat. They gave into their hunger pains because they were weak. Zero self-control.

Cause I'm a hazard to myself
Don't let me get me
I'm my own worst enemy
It's bad when you annoy yourself
So irritating
Don't wanna be my friend no more
I wanna be somebody else

–Pink, "Don't Let Me Get Me"

2 | chicken legs

In my mind, perfectionism is developed during childhood, where one derives a very real sense of pleasure from making a painstaking effort. Pressures from our family, friends, and the media combine to force us into a lifetime of worrying, feeling guilty, and working too hard. I, for one, definitely acquired this characteristic over the years, drowning myself in endless thoughts like "Could I have done that better?" Perhaps I could have, or perhaps I honestly had tried my best. But for some reason, someone else had always done it better than me. Someone else was always more perfect.

Have you ever wondered what it was like to be perfect? My whole life revolved around that thought. All I ever wanted was to be perfect. And the funny thing is I actually thought I could be.

As a fourteen-year-old girl starting high school, life was quite stressful. I had to pick out the perfect outfit for school each day. And I had to worry about my hair, my makeup, and my nails. Plus, on top of all this, I had to worry about my grades. This entailed doing my homework, studying for tests, going to bed at a decent hour...can you just imagine? I was certain I had more to worry about than anyone else. My parents only had to worry about bills, grocery shopping, taxes, mortgages, car insurance, health insurance...But I felt like I had all the worries in the world, as most fourteen-year-olds do.

A new school year was beginning, and this was not just any school year. This was my freshman year in high school, where I'd be introduced to new people and new experiences. I had grown up in one town my entire life. One house. One school system. The people with whom I graduated eighth grade were people I had known since I was four years old. And now I would be attending a new school with many new people to impress and, unfortunately, to compete against.

I had been identified as the "skinny girl" by the end of eighth grade, so now the pressure was on to live up to it. The messages that were written in my eighth grade yearbook made that fact perfectly clear. The first page read, "Jen, you are thin and beautiful. Just remember it." The back inside cover stated, "Don't go on a diet again! You might fade away into nothing!" and "Hey, chicken legs..." and "You better not get any smarter or any thinner. You're too much of both." Now, of course, most teenagers would love to receive these messages in their yearbook. It really makes you feel good about yourself when people go out of their way to pay you a compliment. But these messages were sending me the wrong signal. They were all a reflection of the way they perceived my body to be. It seemed to me that being thin meant being attractive, and this became my measure of human beauty. If I could remain thin, then I would be beautiful. Who would have expected that these remarks would solidify my identity for years to come?

Although I had a label to identify with, I still struggled to find something else that I could be known for. Throughout middle school, aside from taking dance lessons, I also played the piano and the violin. Because I wasn't the best at any of these activities, I became even more involved when I got into high school. In addition to taking dance and piano lessons, I also joined Key Club, played soccer, taught Sunday school at our local church, and sang in the high school choir. And even with all of the activities, I still couldn't find my niche.

Lucky for me, I was still the best at one thing: staying thin. That was definitely my forte. A bus ride on the second day of school supported that conclusion. I was wearing a pair of brown jeans and a ruffled denim shirt that exposed just enough of my stomach to reveal my belly button. My long blonde sprial-permed hair was partially pulled back with a gold barrette, while my pin-straight bangs covered most of my forehead. As the bus pulled into our school's parking lot at approximately seven thirty a.m., I slowly stood up, preparing to exit. While I was lifting my backpack over my shoulders, one of my friends took notice of my flat stomach. "Jen, I can't believe how skinny you are! Uh, I am so jealous!"

"Nice," I thought to myself. "Another person is jealous of my body. I must be doing something right."

As the weeks went on, I continued to receive praise for my thinness, and being successful at my after-school activities became secondary. I enjoyed the attention that I got for my frame and I was determined to keep it that way.

Unfortunately, there were a few drawbacks to my public dieting habit. For one, I wouldn't allow myself to eat at parties—or even in public, for that matter. I couldn't let people actually see me eat. That would be defeating the purpose. I wouldn't be viewed as having control, which is what I so desperately desired. They all envied my willpower. I had to remain in control, because that was the one thing that no one else had. But at the same time, they all had happiness. They all had fun gatherings, which usually included food of some kind. Whether it was pizza, Chinese food, birthday cake, or even dinner at a restaurant, my friends had fun losing that control. And while I was supposed to be sharing their fun, I was feeling isolated instead. Because I had given myself no choice but to remain in control, I couldn't allow myself to have fun. Although physically I would be present, emotionally and mentally I was withdrawn.

By midyear, I had become extremely detached from my social network. I was extremely isolated from my friends and family. I had convinced myself that I was still very happy because I was skinny. Thinness equaled happiness, at least that's what the media depicted. However, deep down, I knew that I truly wasn't content. I just didn't know what I was feeling. I was completely numb. I wouldn't allow myself to be sad, scared, or angry. Although I truly did experience all of these feelings, I didn't want to express them so I forced myself to appear happy at all times.

But although I looked happy on the outside, my true feelings were bottled up on the inside. As my anger, frustration, guilt, and sadness accumulated month after month, I began to realize how much I hated wearing the mask of happiness. I wanted to be able to share my pain. I wanted to tell people when I was angry, and I wanted the freedom to express my frustrations. But I couldn't. I wouldn't allow it. I had to pretend I was perfect. I received so much attention for that trait. Perfection made me feel special, just not special enough.

One night I was studying in my room with my door locked so my sister couldn't bother me. As usual, I became distracted from the material I was reading and began to daydream. Earlier in the week, my science teacher had told us a story about her ex-roommate who tried slitting her wrists. For some reason, this story intrigued me. "How could someone inflict physical pain on themselves? What on earth would they gain from such an experience?" I thought to myself.

I was curious enough, and bored for that matter, to try it myself. I picked up a compass that was resting peacefully in my pencil holder, paused for a brief second and then gently scraped it against my pale skin. For the first time in a long time, I was able to feel pain. Surprisingly, it was amazing. I enjoyed feeling the pain from the compass because I was unable to feel all of the other emotional pain I had bottled up inside. So I scraped my arm again, this time a little bit harder than the first. It still felt good and I began to wonder if I could actually go through with slitting my wrist. People would think I was crazy but I still wanted to try it. I continued scraping my left wrist, over and over and over again. I began to see blood and tiny pieces of skin accumulate on top of my desk. "I don't really want to die right now, do I?" I asked myself.

No, I didn't really want to die. As soon as I realized that, I stopped. By this point my wrist was bleeding profusely, and I needed to apply pressure to the wound. What had I just done?

As I secretly wiped the blood off the compass with a tissue and rinsed my wrist in the bathroom sink, I started to wonder about why I had just done what I did. Was that normal? No, I don't think so. I don't know anyone else that punctures their skin for fun. But why did I like it so much? Why did I like hurting myself? It was odd and intriguing at the same time. Part of me wanted to show someone, but if I did I would definitely get forced into seeing a psychologist, which was last on my list of things to do. As a result I decided to keep it a secret. I put Band-Aids over it and wore only long sleeve shirts for the next few days. Luckily, it was in the middle of March, so long sleeves were still the fashion of choice.

About a week after the compass incident, I was in health class when one of my good friends, Sheila, took notice of my wrist. I had taken the Band-Aids off, as the scars were beginning to scab and heal. While sitting at my desk, about the third row back, I quickly took out my planner to add a few details before class started, not realizing that my scabs were showing for all to see. As Sheila walked down the aisle to her desk in back of mine, she loudly questioned, "Jen, what happened to your wrist?"

I quickly replied that my dog had jumped up and scratched me. Not the most convincing answer, but it was the best I could do under pressure. Although she seemed to believe me, she replied, "Oh, I thought you tried to slit your wrists or something," with a slight smirk on her face. For the most part, I wanted to believe that she trusted my answer, but there was a small part of me that wanted her to figure out the truth. Perhaps it was because I wanted more attention or perhaps it was because I wanted her to help me. Regardless, I continued my day with a scarred wrist that constantly reminded me that something wasn't right.

Although the scars on my wrist were healing and the physical pain had subsided, my emotional pain continued to build. As the weeks went on, I cared less about my well-being and more about my physical appearance. The continuous comments regarding my thinness were extremely gratifying. I stuck to a rigid daily exercise routine consisting of sit-ups, push-ups, leg-lifts, and running. Soon my appearance became my number one priority. Based on what I read in magazines and saw on television, worrying about your weight and calorie consumption was completely normal. I had become brainwashed into thinking that starvation was standard.

In fact, I could never turn on *Beverly Hills, 90210,* my favorite television show, without one of the girls mentioning her hair, clothes, or body. Occasionally, one of the episodes would focus on a serious issue such as eating disorders or alcoholism with the intent of teaching kids a lesson. However, viewers that suffered from the exploited problems could get the wrong message and gain new ideas instead. Sometimes, the noble intentions of the producers would backfire, which is exactly what happened to me.

It was April 1993 when *Beverly Hills, 90210* aired an episode about a character named Kelly who began abusing diet pills. In the beginning of the episode she complained about how fat she was and her need to go on a diet. She then showed her friend Donna the diet pills she bought. Instead of taking one or two a day, she was taking four at a time and lived entirely on coffee. Towards the end of the episode, at her surprise birthday party, she passed out in the bathroom and was taken to the emergency room. After a few chats with her mother and friends, she swore to start eating and join an eating disorders support group in order to fix her problem. By the next week's episode, all was forgotten. Although most viewers learned that diet pills were bad for you, I wasn't one of them. I immediately thought, "Hey, what a good idea!" The next day, I went to our local pharmacy and purchased two boxes of Dexatrim, hoping that I would get fast results.

I started taking two pills at a time, three times a day. My diet consisted of a granola bar for breakfast, no lunch, and a small dinner. The reasoning behind the "no lunch" policy was because I wanted my friends and classmates to see the control I had. This was my main way of receiving attention and feeling special since I failed to take notice at the praise for my good grades or participation in extracurricular activities. The only praise I seemed to take notice of was that on my body. Boys taking notice of my abnormally skinny stomach and girls being jealous of my thin physique seemed to be the only comments I cared about. Perhaps it was because I was the *only* one who had this control. There were many people that achieved high academic performance and many who sang well and danced well. But I was the *only* one who could diet well at my school and I wanted to make sure that people knew it.

After a few weeks of taking Dexatrim, I made it a point to announce my diet pill usage. I told a few friends, who at the time found it a bit disturbing but didn't say much. Of course, they told me the pills weren't good for me, but did they think I was actually going to listen? Hah! They were just jealous that I had the determination to loose weight and they didn't. One of my good friends, Kim, even tried the reverse psychology approach. One day in the locker room she came up to me with an envelope stuffed with ten dollars. She said, "Jen, I want you to buy me two packages of whatever diet pills you bought. If you can take them, so can I."

I gave the money right back to her. "I'm not going to buy these for you. You can't take them. They're not healthy for you," I whispered, trying not to cause a scene. Deep down I knew they weren't healthy for me either. But I casually ignored that fact for the sake of losing more weight. Of course, I couldn't have someone else starting the same habit. This was my special something and no one was going to take that away.

I continued to live up to my identity throughout sophomore year, which was full of many parties—particularly sweet sixteens. And at each one, without fail, my friends commented on the food that was on my plate. Of course, I only ate fruit, if anything, at these events. I could never let anyone see me eat anything fattening. There were a few occasions where I actually contemplated having a piece of cake, but before I could even request a piece someone would make a comment like "Look, Jen. Its cake. Doesn't it look good? Oh, I'm sorry. I forgot. You can't have cake. It has too many calories for you." At that point, I felt like I would not be living up to my identity if I had a piece. I would feel like such a failure. I would feel like I wasn't living up to everyone's expectations. I couldn't do that. I couldn't disappoint everyone. I couldn't disappoint myself. So, I continued to limit my food intake, especially when in public.

My control and perseverance paid off that fall when I was nominated for Sophomore Homecoming Princess. Although it was assumed the nominations were based on academic achievement, school spirit, and inner beauty, I believed it was for one reason and one reason only. I must have been nominated because I was thin. Ironically, when it came time to decide on what to wear to the Homecoming ceremony, I became overwhelmed. Underweight at only 110 pounds, I still thought that I had huge thighs and needed to somehow hide them. Eventually, I decided on a pair of stretch pants with a baggy sweater on top that concealed my massive butt.

At the homecoming selection ceremony, I timidly stood in my baggy sweater, under the irrational belief that everyone was staring at my thighs, when in fact they were just waiting for the results. I won the title of Sophomore Homecoming Princess that year and no one could have prepared me for that moment. For a quick second, I felt special, and for once, not because I was skinny. I only wish that feeling had lasted longer.

After the homecoming win, my eating habits slowly began to change. My social calendar became unusually busy, and I was finding it harder to make up excuses for not eating in public. And the more I ate, the more my body started working against me. It demanded food, and my superhuman willpower diminished. Even though I wouldn't eat in public, I gave myself permission to eat at home. Perhaps I missed the taste of the foods I used to love—ice cream, french fries, pizza, nachos, potato chips. There were so many "bad" foods that I was missing out on. Part of me broke down that year, and I decided that it was okay to eat these foods as long as I starved myself for the rest of the day. I stuck to a similar regimen—a small breakfast and no lunch. However, when I got home from school, usually around three o'clock, I would break down and lose my control. I'd be starving and would reach for any food that was available, usually something microwavable like pizza or french fries. I would try to eat a smaller dinner to make up for it, but sometimes I just couldn't resist. The more I allowed myself to eat, the more I wanted. At this rate, my weight rapidly increased to 128 pounds over the next few months. Food had now become a source of comfort.

Although I was finally eating on a regular basis, I remained only comfortable eating in isolation. When I ate alone, I could eat and feel free. I could never let anyone see me with my guard down. I could never let anyone see me as a failure, a girl who is supposed to suppress her appetite but who divulges in these delicacies in private. I don't know what I would do if anyone saw me eat like that. I felt like a disgusting pig!

And the funny thing was, I wasn't even doing anything that abnormal. Eating isn't abnormal. Eating a small plate of french fries on occasion is legal, isn't it? For most people, sure it is. But since I had been staying away from these fattening foods for so long, people thought it was abnormal for me to be eating them. Even if I tried to eat normally in a public situation, I received comments such as, "You're actually going to eat *that*? I can't believe it! That has too many calories for you." Even my grandmother would make comments like that. It made me assume I was doing something wrong. I was Jennifer Otto, a.k.a. "the thin girl." I was the one who wasn't supposed to eat "bad" foods. Everyone else was allowed to eat these foods, but I wasn't. I was *special*. I had superhuman willpower.

So I tried to stick to it. Eating alone, and not eating in public. These were the rules. I would eat something small for lunch, like an apple, since I was with classmates at that time. But when I got home and was alone, I'd allow my hunger to take over. It was almost like an out-of-body experience. I became this ferocious beast that would scarf down anything that I could get my hands on, such as an entire bag of nachos with Cheez Wiz. This pattern continued for months. Eating became a secret. My life revolved around food. I looked forward to the moments where I could indulge in "bad" food, which meant I looked forward to being alone. I looked forward to the isolation. I looked forward to my parents staying at work late and my sister going to her friends' houses. That meant more time for me to eat.

During those weak moments, when I wasn't thinking about the calories, I felt free. Free of all my pain and sorrow. But once I was finished and my stomach was uncomfortably full, I would become overwhelmed with guilt and anger. How could I lose that control? How had I become such a failure? I was no longer the perfect anorexic. I was no longer in control. I had lost my special attribute. After my binges, I had nothing.

I'd then spend the next few days trying to lose the weight that I was convinced I had gained from the binge. I'd live on gum and diet soda. In my mind, the only beverage that anyone should ever drink was water or diet soda. They're the only logical liquids to drink for one simple reason: they contain 0 calories. Why drink something that has calories like juice, milk, lemonade, or iced tea? If you're going to consume the calories, you should really make them count. It doesn't make any sense to waste precious calories with just a simple beverage. If you are going to indulge, have something worthwhile, like a few potato chips or something. Never drink calories. It's the only logical thing to do.

That February, my friend Melissa and I had planned our annual Miss USA sleepover. Every year ever since I could remember, Melissa and I would get together to watch the Miss USA pageant. We would begin the evening with makeovers, which consisted of muddy mint green face masks, cucumber blindfolds, manicures, hair curlers, and heavy makeup, with an emphasis on blue eye shadow. For that one night every year, we'd pretend to be supermodels. Our mothers would even take pictures of us in a bunch of silly poses.

After our glamorous transformations, usually around nine p.m., we would put on our pj's and snuggle up to watch the pageant, complete with notepads for tracking the scores for our favorite choices. Our goal would be to choose the winner right from the start. That year, neither of us chose the girl who won, but we soon were distracted by the toll-free number that flashed on the screen. They were looking for contestants for the next Miss Teen USA pageant. Because it had always been our dreams to become Miss USA, we decided to jot the number down. We called the very next day and they immediately sent us applications. The pageant officials selected thirty girls out of two hundred that year to compete in the pageant, and my friend Melissa and I were two of them.

Over the next few months, we raised money, bought various outfits for the event, and even had our pictures printed in the newspaper. This pageant would just be another means for receiving attention for my body. At this point, my weight had stabilized at a healthy amount, around 120 pounds, and I felt pretty healthy too. I became so focused on the competition that I had lost my focus on the food. My eating habits began to level out as I tried to eat healthier going into the competition. I didn't want to starve myself to the point where I'd pass out on stage, but I also didn't want to gorge myself into being a plus-size contestant.

The pageant finally came at the beginning of September, and of course, I compared my body to everyone else's throughout the entire weekend. I also watched to see what every other girl was eating. Contrary to my own beliefs, I found that most of the girls were eating much more than I was. It was astounding! One girl actually ate a salad, a sandwich, and a piece of fruit! I couldn't believe it. Others were eating pizza and, much to my surprise, drinking regular Coke with all the empty calories that came with it. Weren't they worried about all those calories? I didn't understand how they could eat normally like that and not freak out about it. I tried to eat with them, but the entire time I just kept thinking that they all must be staring at me. I was very intimidated.

The finals came on Sunday, and when they announced the top ten, my name was not called. But I noticed that, somehow, all the skinny girls were called. I assumed they were called simply because they were skinnier than I was. I was just too fat to be picked. This conclusion was just the motivation I needed to catapult me back to starvation. If I wasn't skinny enough to win a silly beauty pageant, then I wasn't skinny enough to live.

Shortly after the Miss Teen USA pageant were the Homecoming Nominations once again. If I was going to be picked as Junior Homecoming Princess, I was going to have to lose some weight. It was obvious that beauty contests were only judged by one thing—weight. I was determined to lose at least 10 pounds, which would bring me back down to 110. Getting down to 110 pounds became my first priority. Not school. Not family. Not friends. Not church. It was losing weight. I finally took back the control and was on a quest to find my thin self again—or a thinner self, for that matter.

I know a girl who should never be alone
I know a girl who should never be alone
She's in danger to herself
And I'm worried about her health
She's got a problem
And she's gonna do something dumb…

–Fountains of Wayne, "She's Got a Problem"

3 | golden influence

"Did you see that TV movie last night with Tracey Gold?" my friend asked me as we were walking out of precalculus class.

"Yeah, I saw parts of it," I muttered under my breath. I casually paused in order to hear her next comment on the TV special.

"I can't believe how thin she looked. When she was standing in front of the mirror in that black dress, she looked just like a skeleton. It was so gross!" she exclaimed.

"Yeah, she did, I guess," I quickly replied. "I gotta go. See ya."

As I swiftly walked away, I pictured that same scene in my mind. I didn't think she looked too thin. I actually thought she looked perfect. It was cool that you could see her ribs sticking out. I wanted mine to do that.

I had actually seen the entire movie from beginning to end. I even taped it so I could watch it over and over again. When I had initially seen the advertisements for the movie in the October 2 issue of *TV Guide*, I cut them out and saved them in my planner. I didn't want to miss the drama about the girl suffering from anorexia. I had made sure all my homework was done and I was ready for bed when the movie entitled *For the Love of Nancy* aired at nine p.m. on Sunday, October 2, 1994.

As Nancy, the main character played by Tracey Gold, demonstrated self-destructive rituals and obsessions relating to food, I carefully observed and made mental notes in the back of my mind. This fictional portrayal wasn't showing me what *not* to do; it was showing me what *to* do. During those two hours, I learned many new tricks and habits I could use in order to obtain my goal. By combining a strict diet consisting of nothing for breakfast, a granola bar for a mid-morning snack, nothing for lunch, a normal dinner, and five diet pills a day, I was on my way to a thinner Jen. A better, more perfect, Jen, in my mind.

A few weeks after the movie had aired, the nominations for Homecoming Princess were announced, and they included my name. I figured that I had even a better chance to win this year, since I had lost some weight and was close to about 116 pounds. This was 4 pounds less than what I had weighed the year before, so I was obviously better looking. In my mind, the less I weighed, the better I looked.

Unfortunately, it obviously didn't make too much of a difference to everyone else. I ended up losing the Junior Homecoming Princess title that year to a prettier girl who probably weighed less than me. I'm positive that she weighed less than me. She just had to. It wasn't fair. She was more popular and really skinny. I didn't care so much about the popularity. Screw being popular. All I cared about was being the skinniest. Losing this title just gave me more drive and desire to obtain that goal.

My new target weight became 105. That seemed like a reasonable goal. Then, perhaps, I'd have a chance at becoming Homecoming Queen my Senior Year.

"Steve, can you grab me a cup of ice while you're in there?" I pleasantly asked.

"Sure, but what do you need ice for?" he countered.

"Don't worry about it!" I proclaimed, half joking but half serious at the same time. "Just do it!"

Steve was one of my good friends. I sat with him every day for lunch in the cafeteria, along with Maggie, Natalie and Carly. After I lost the Homecoming Princess race and began my hard-core quest for weight-loss, I stopped eating granola bars and decided I would only eat ice for lunch. Ice was great because it gave me something to chew on without consuming any calories. However, I couldn't bring myself to go into the cafeteria line to get it. The food smelled too good, even in my high school cafeteria. The warm waft of greasy fries was too overwhelming for me to bear.

Steve finally made it out of the lunch line and back to our table, clutching onto a large cup of ice cubes that he hurriedly dropped on the table in front of me.

"Is that all you're eating?" he inquired. "That can't be all that you are eating for lunch."

"I had a big breakfast this morning. It's hard to last until noon with only a small bowl of cereal," I retorted. "I'm going to eat lunch when I get home. No worries."

"Alright, suit yourself," he replied. "There's no way I'm waiting until three to eat lunch. I'm starving!"

I'm sure Steve and the others didn't believe me, but I needed to say something to justify my behavior. At this point, the last thing I was worrying about was what people were thinking. All I cared about was losing weight.

Weeks went by and my lunches of ice became normal. My friends would usually grab the table directly in the middle of the cafeteria, in between the cheerleaders and the artsy kids. I would sit at the table, usually towards the end of the group, as far away from their food as possible. I'd chomp on my ice as they ate their turkey sandwiches, french fries, and pizza. Occasionally, I would cave in and have a few fries in order to appear somewhat normal, and in hopes that my friends would believe my little charade.

After a while, they finally stopped questioning my ice habit. On the positive side, I didn't have to deal with all the inquiries and lies. However, on the negative side, I felt like I could never bring or buy a normal lunch because that would then be seen as unusual. Again I would have to deal with the questioning. Not only that, but I felt as if I would be seen as a failure. I would be seen as someone who had lost her control, and the most important thing to me was that people could see I had control. That was who I was. I just couldn't let them down. I just couldn't.

Now that lunches were taken care of, I needed to somehow dodge our family dinners as well. Ideally, I wanted to find a solution that didn't require me to eat a thing. I needed an excuse to eat alone, so I could easily rid the food without anyone seeing. And then, within the blink of an eye, it came to me. Studying would be my excuse. It was genius!

I was a junior in high school and always had a ton of homework to do. I was working the hardest I had ever worked since I was getting ready to apply to college. Therefore, I made it seem as though my studies were of the utmost importance. In the interest of saving time, I convinced my mom to let me eat dinner in my room so I could study at the same time. Of course, without giving it a second thought, she fell for it.

With this clever strategy, I could bring my dinner upstairs to my room and, moments later, quietly flush my food down the toilet. It was a win/win situation in my opinion. My parents would believe I was eating my meals, and I would get away with not eating a thing. It was the perfect scenario. I was finally skipping all three meals on a daily basis. I would be on my way to 105 pounds in no time.

As the holidays drew near, I began to develop anxiety over all the gatherings I would have to attend and the large feasts that were associated with each. I had mastered the art of escaping my meals on a daily basis, but the holidays were different. With my family, they usually involved long sit-down meals with my grandparents. It would certainly be difficult to get out of those situations without having to eat something.

There were nights I couldn't sleep because I was too busy scheming and calculating my plan to circumvent Thanksgiving Dinner. There was no way I was going to be able to take my food upstairs and flush it down the toilet like I normally did. I knew I would have to stay at the table and socialize. As a result, I decided my strategy would be to take as little food as possible, load up on veggies and salad, and spread it around on my plate so it looked like I had more than in reality.

Thanksgiving finally arrived, and as usual, my grandparents and great-aunt came over to our house for the festivities. I somehow got stuck sitting at the head of the table in between my grandfather and my sister, with my plate in plain view for everyone to see. After my father said grace, the food began to circulate counter clock-wise around the table and anxiety immediately set in. I could feel the sweat forming in the palms of my hands as I took the basket of dinner rolls my grandfather had handed me. I wanted to eat everything but nothing at the same time.

The food smelled so good, but I knew I shouldn't eat it. I would gain so much weight if I had a normal serving. So I tried as hard as I could to stick to my plan. I took enough salad to fill up half my plate, intentionally overlooking the individual salad bowl sitting next to my plate. Hopefully, no one would notice. In addition to the salad, I took a couple pieces of turkey and then filled the rest of my plate with my mom's favorite vegetable combination, peas and carrots. Luckily, everyone seemed to be in such deep conversation that no one took notice of my carb-free dish.

I reluctantly took bite after bite. Overwhelmed with anguish, I could feel the fat piling onto my bones while everyone else watched. I took the smallest possible bites and spread my food around on my plate to create a perception that I ate more than I actually did. Conversations were happening all around me but I heard nothing. All I could hear were the voices in my head. They were telling me to slow down and take smaller bites. I wasn't even allowed to look at the bowl of mashed potatoes as those were completely off-limits. The voices and commands were extremely overwhelming. It was complete chaos as the thoughts raced one after the other in my mind. All I desired was to take the silver serving spoon and start shoveling those garlic-infused potatoes dripping with butter into my mouth. If no one was around, I probably would end up doing just that. And I'd almost certainly eat the entire bowl.

Luckily, I was able to remain in control for the entire dinner. I finished most of the turkey I had taken on my plate. I felt uncomfortably full and nauseous even though I had only consumed what would be considered a small-sized lunch for most people. How could they make me do this? How could my parents just sit there while I was blowing up into a blimp? And the thing that was so unfair about all of this was they could all eat a ton of food and not gain one pound or look any different. But with each bite I took, I got heavier and heavier. It just wasn't fair.

Soon after we finished Thanksgiving dinner, I raced to the upstairs bathroom so I could weigh myself and calculate the damage that had been done. 110 pounds. Oh good Lord! That was three more pounds than the day before. I knew it! Eating was bad! Food was horrible! That did it. I would have to restrict even more and I would have to take more diet pills. The more, the better, in my mind. So I willingly increased my dosage to four diet pills three times daily, which made for twelve pills a day, eleven more than the suggested amount. Yet over the month of December, I watched my weight plummet to 103. Apparently, my increased dosage wasn't such a bad idea.

Although I was happy with the results, the side effects that came with the weight loss were not so desirable. Each day I felt faint from the lack of nutrition, and the pills were causing me to feel overstrung. I was shivering at one moment and sweating the next. Why was this happening? I could barely make it through each day. I had zero energy. But as soon as I stepped on that scale and saw that I lost weight, I got the greatest adrenaline rush ever! No one could ever understand what a high it was to see the numbers go down. It was my greatest accomplishment. It was the only thing I lived for. And if I didn't lose weight, I would try even harder. I would exercise every night in my bedroom, alone. I chewed gum. I ate ice. Whatever it was going to take, I would keep losing weight.

"Are you going to Katie's house for New Years Eve?" Jamie asked me.

"Of course," I answered. "I can't wait."

I honestly was looking forward to the party, just not the eating part of it. The festivities started at six, so I conveniently arrived at seven thirty, which gave me the excuse that I had already eaten dinner with my family. When I arrived, there was a huge buffet of food set up in Katie's dining room. Everyone was sitting around leaning over their plastic dishes, eating ziti, bread, salad, and cookies. For most, the food was a highlight but for me, it was just a distraction.

I quickly announced I had already eaten dinner but, without even thinking, snagged an italian cookie. I couldn't resist. It smelled so good and my body was desperately seeking something that would give it energy. The icing immediately began to melt in my hand while I stared at the sprinkles on top, wondering how many calories it was going to cost me. One cookie couldn't have more than a hundred calories, I thought to myself. I hadn't eaten anything all day, so I was able to justify it. I quickly inhaled it, hoping no one was watching. I didn't want anyone to see me giving up my control.

And just like that, it was gone in an instant. I wanted more but resisted the temptation. One cookie was plenty. That was my binge for the week. No more food was allowed to cross my lips, I told myself. I was done. Diet Coke for the rest of the night. Without delay I jumped up, got a large red Solo cup, and filled it with ice and diet soda. I washed down what remained of the cookie and quickly distracted myself by chatting with the other girls. I didn't want to think about that cookie ever again.

Many of the girls made comments about my weight that night, even though I was wearing baggy jeans and an untucked oversized button-down shirt. Of course, I loved the attention. However, I still couldn't see what they were seeing. One of Katie's living room walls was covered from floor to ceiling in mirrors. As I stood in front of the wall talking to Jamie, I couldn't help but inspect every inch of my body. My thighs were huge, my butt was unbelievably big, and my stomach could still be flatter. If I could just lose a few more pounds, I'd be satisfied. I couldn't wait until I reached the 100-pound barrier. What a rush it would be to weigh less than 100 pounds. Double-digits were my ideal.

Unfortunately, my plans finally came to a halt. I returned to high school after our Christmas vacation on January 3. Early that morning, I took a total of ten diet pills. I presumed I should increase my dosage, as my body was probably getting used to my usual four-pill regimen. I left the house with a piece of toast that my mother had shoved in my hands on my way out the door to the bus stop. I threw it to the birds halfway up the street.

Once I had been at school for a few hours, I started to feel some pretty severe side effects from the diet pills. I couldn't concentrate in class. I was freezing, yet the back of my neck was full of sweat. I felt nauseous and faint. There was absolutely no way I could stay and sit in class.

Not wasting another minute, I wandered down to the nurse's office and immediately asked to lie down. When she asked how I was feeling, I told her my symptoms, but I obviously left out the fact that I had taken ten diet pills that morning. Without knowing about the pills, it sounded as if I had the flu. She proceeded to take my temperature, a measly 97.5 degrees. Since I didn't have a fever, there was no need to send me home. However, she allowed me to rest there for a while until I felt better. I stared at the cinderblock wall with my back sunken into the hunter green leather chaise. I desperately wanted to fall asleep while my body wore off the effects from the pills. My heart was racing yet I had absolutely no energy. I just felt terrible. And I had no one to blame but myself. Right then and there, I swore I would never take those pills again.

As soon as I got home, I threw on a pair of sweats and got into bed. As I lay there under the warm covers, I started to realize the damage I was doing to my body. Did I want to feel this way for the rest of my life? Did I want to isolate myself? Did I really want to miss out on the great-tasting foods that all of my friends always raved about? Why was I doing this? There had to be a way that I could have all the energy and fun that my friends had, yet still lose weight at the same time. There just had to be.

I stared at the ceiling in silence. All I wanted at that moment was for someone to comfort me. I just wanted someone to tell me that everything was going to be okay. Luckily, within the hour, my mother arrived home from work. As usual, she wandered upstairs to see me and found me crying, bundled up in blankets in my bed.

I broke down and told her everything. I told her how I was feeling due to the diet pills. I also told her about my fear of eating. She immediately suggested that I needed help and took me to the hospital nearby to have me checked out. I was skeptical but relieved at the same time. I could finally get some help. As long as no one made me eat, I would be fine.

Diary Entry: 1/3/95

Today, I did one of the hardest things that I ever had to do. When mom came home from work at five, she found me shivering, cold in bed with many blankets wrapped around me. I was crying uncontrollably. She asked me what was wrong. I told her I was scared and confused. I know I'm anorexic. Starving myself is the easiest and fastest way to lose weight.

At first I was hungry all of the time. I figured diet pills would be the best way to control my appetite. Well, they worked. It all began in October. I watched the movie on TV starring Tracey Gold. It was a true story of some teenage girl who had been starving herself to become thin. It looked like a good idea to me. Ever since then, I have been stuffing myself with diet pills instead of food. Within seven weeks I have lost 25 pounds. Beginning at 125, I am now at 100 pounds. After Christmas I realized I wasn't losing any more weight, so I took more pills to lose weight faster. Well, it didn't work. Instead, I felt weaker as the days passed. I was always cold and constantly forgetting things. I also was finding it hard to concentrate. After I told mom everything, she took me to Overlook Hospital.

The hospital was hell. I kept inspecting myself in one of the long mirrors hanging in the ER. Even though my black stretch pants were hanging off of me, I could still see blubber surrounding my thighs. I felt that being there was nonsense. I was too fat to be anorexic. Didn't you have to weigh like 60 pounds in order to be really sick? I mean, c'mon. Please. I would never get like that.

As soon as I realized that I might have to get help, I pictured myself gaining 50 pounds. Getting help meant getting fat, right? No way! No way would I ever agree to gain weight! That would be, like, going against my own religion or something. It would be like committing a crime! At this point, I would feel less guilty about robbing a bank than eating a french fry.

After five hours of blood tests and conversations with the doctors, the hospital recommended a clinic, which specialized in eating disorders. Mom promised me she would call first thing tomorrow morning. I'm sure it was a relief for her to finally hear me admit that I had a problem. I had finally given her permission to get me help.

Diary Entry: 1/4/95

At eight a.m., mom called St. Clare's hospital in Booton, NJ. The intake specialists talked to both mom and me over the phone and we made an appointment for tomorrow. I am supposed to have an interview with one of the doctors and a tour of the clinic. I am scared but at the same time grateful. After seeing programs based on the dangers of diet pills, especially Dexatrim, I am just happy to be alive. On the other hand, I am scared that I can't eat, even though I want to. I hope this place will be able to help me with my problem. I don't know what to expect. How long will I have to stay there? I wonder what the people are like. I'm sure they are friendly and helpful. At least it sounded that way on the phone. We'll see tomorrow.

Diary Entry: 1/5/95

I went back to school today but only stayed until twelve thirty. Mom picked me up and took me over to St. Clare's Hospital. When we arrived, one of the eating disorder specialists began our visit by giving us a tour of the unit. The "ED Wing," as they called it, seemed very isolated but safe. Everything was locked, including the bathrooms.

As we began our journey down the long corridor, we first passed the bedrooms, which were painted a pale violet, accented with plum-colored curtains and floral bedspreads. The dining area was next, much smaller than I imagined, followed by the payphones. I was told there were restrictions on when phone calls could and could not be made, and they had a strict limit of three calls per day. Next, she showed us the bathrooms. As she began unlocking the door, she informed me of yet another rule. Patients had to request a nurse to open the bathroom when they needed it. The nurse would monitor their usage in case they tried throwing up, which by the way, I have tried but have had little success. Next door to the bathrooms was the TV lounge, where a group therapy session was currently in progress. As I peeked through the door, I noticed one girl had a tube up her nose. I later found out that she wasn't eating and needed to be force-fed. It made me realize that I never wanted to get like that and that I truly wanted to get better. Overall, this place was a little scary-looking, but I wasn't against it. If I had to, I'd stay.

The specialist then took us back to her office, where she explained a patient's daily routine. I would have three meals and two snacks each day. This seemed extremely overwhelming. Right now, I'm having a hard time with just the one meal a day. We would also have group meetings, one-on-one counseling, and sessions with the nutritionist. We would also have to be weighed every morning. On the whole, except for the bathroom monitoring, everything was as I expected.

Then, without any warning, she asked if she could weigh me, in clothes and all! She could have at least let me go to the bathroom first! Well, I stepped up on the scale and much to my disappointment, it read 100 pounds. I was very upset that I hadn't gone under 100 yet.

We quickly returned to her desk and she proceeded to tell me and mom that they typically do not admit patients that weigh as much as I do. "We just do an intensive day treatment program for those who are not in any physical danger," she said.

Therefore, I wasn't sick enough, in my mind. My first instinct was to lose more weight so I could get more attention and be admitted full-time. So I'm obviously trying to run away from reality, but why? What am I afraid of? Why don't I want to stay at home? Perhaps it's my family. Or my classmates. Who knows? All I know is that I want to get away for a very long time and this is my only way of achieving that goal.

After a few more interviews and tours at a variety of hospitals, my mother and I chose one that was located forty-five minutes away called the Carrier Clinic in Belle Mead, NJ. I was happy with this choice—they didn't monitor you in the bathroom at this place. I don't think that I could have handled that lack of privacy.

Because I still weighed in at a whopping 100 pounds, I was only admitted into the outpatient program. I would attend five days a week from eight a.m. until six p.m. I would eat all three meals at the clinic, and the rule was that we had to finish all of our food before leaving the table. I had no idea how I would ever eat that much food! I had the weekend to get used to the idea, because Monday it would start.

Diary Entry: 1/7/95

Today, I woke up with one thing on my mind. Food. How much was I going to eat today? Although I was not hungry at all, Mom made me eat at eleven a.m. She barely managed to get me to have a piece of toast and a few sips of juice. It tasted good. However, I knew it would make me gain weight. I excused myself from the table and did as many sit-ups as I could in my room.

Around four p.m., I began getting a little hungry. Mom made me have a plain piece of bread. She also decided to run to the market to get me some lemon pudding, since it was the only thing I could agree on eating. I ate a small cup of the pudding and realized that my stomach was aching. If I couldn't even eat a little pudding, how was I going to finish an entire meal? I feel like I just gained fifty pounds! We'll see tomorrow when I'm forced to be weighed. It's so frustrating because I know I have to eat in order to get healthy, but I'd rather just be skinny.

I did get weighed the next morning, but I wasn't allowed to see the results. This was extremely frustrating, to say the least. I was dying to know if I had gained weight, as I was certain I must have from eating that toast and pudding the day before. My medical team, as they called themselves, put me on a 1200-calorie-per-day diet. I knew I would definitely gain a lot of weight on this diet since it was at least twice as many calories as I was consuming at that point.

My first few hours at the center were spent in one-on-one introductory meetings with my medical team. I met with my therapist, psychologist and a nutritionist. All of these meetings went pretty much as expected – me giving the same monotonous summary of my life story while being stared at in silence. I had to do everything in my power to keep the eye-rolling to a minimum, since I couldn't quite figure out how these sessions were going to solve all of my problems. It was going to take a lot more than some repetivite story-telling to get me to eat without analyzing every morsel. But I was still willing to give it a chance since I really didn't have any other option.

Finally, lunchtime came, and I was forced to eat an entire peanut butter sandwich, a bowl of fruit salad, a package of carrot sticks, and a half glass of skim milk. It was ridiculously overwhelming and most certainly did not seem rational. No normal person would ever eat this amount of food in one sitting, I thought to myself. It took me over an hour to finish it all. Afterwards, all I could think of was dinner. There was no way I was going to be able to eat another full meal like that in four hours.

During those four hours, aside from our group therapy session, I met Michelle, the other outpatient who came every day, 5 days a week.

"How long have you been here?" I asked. It seemed like she had been here for a while.

"A week and a half, but this isn't my first time here," she responded. "This is my third enrollment in the program within the last four years. I can't stop relapsing."

My therapist had mentioned setbacks earlier that morning. "Recovery isn't a straight road," she said, "but instead, a very bumpy one. The bumps start out pretty frequently in your journey but decrease in size and frequency over time." Michelle was now my living proof of this theory.

It turned out that Michelle and I had lots in common. This made me nervous, as I did not want to be returning back to Carrier for another visit. Once would hopefully be enough therapy for me.

We developed a bond right from the beginning since we were both dealing with so many of the same issues. The conversation flowed effortlessly, like we were old friends catching up over coffee. Talking to Michelle was much easier than talking to my therapist who didn't seem like she could relate at all.

By mid-afernoon, we started comparing our regular rituals and daily habits, along with the side-effects of each.

"Is your hair falling out?" I questioned. "Mine is coming out all the time, especially in the shower. Like, in clumps."

"Oh yeah, absolutely!" she enthusiastically replied. "It's horrible. What about muscle spasms? Do you ever have those? Sometimes I'll be sitting or just lying in bed and my leg will start twitching. It's the strangest thing."

"I have noticed that too," I whispered. "But I never really associated that with my anorexia." For some reason, admitting that I was anorexic was easier when I whispered. "I just assumed it happened to everyone. I'm more freaked out about my lack of energy and having the chills constantly. It's like I'm coming down with the flu, but I never really actually get it, ya know?"

"Yep, I feel the same way," she concurred. "I never wanted to recognize the relation between starving myself with all of these issues, but once I started eating again, I could clearly notice a difference. The lack of nutrition definitely took a toll that I just couldn't appreciate until I got healthier."

It was amazing that someone else was feeling the same way I was. It was scary but reassuring at the same time. I had never really acknowledged everything that the anorexia was doing to my body. This conversation was finally making me realize all the damage I was doing. I was terrified.

Unfortunately, there was something else that Michelle was dealing with due to the anorexia that I had yet to come across. Michelle had developed major heart problems. Because she had been starving herself for so long, over ten years at this point, her heart was extremely weak. The lack of nutrients had finally caught up with her and had caused her muscles to diminish. She had to constantly go for tests to make sure that her heart was stabilized. This is what scared me the most.

I didn't want to end up having heart problems—especially before the age of eighteen! But there was no way I could ever get that bad. I would know when to stop. She weighed much less than I did. I would never get to be as skinny as her because I knew that she looked sickly. My intentions were never to look sickly; I just wanted to be 'fashionably skinny.'

Although I thought this sounded rational, deep down I knew that I was a little crazy. Part of me was jealous of her. Part of me was jealous of her weight, and part of me honestly wanted to be as skinny as her. Part of me was even jealous of the attention she was getting for having the heart problem. It was crazy. It was insane. What was I thinking?

As the weeks went by, the days grew shorter and the nights grew longer. I was no longer dreading going to the hospital but instead, I was dreading going home. At home, I was on my own with no one to monitor my intake. But at the hospital, I felt safe. There, I was in a secure world full where all of my food was measured for me. There, I knew I couldn't binge. At the hospital, I finally felt in control.

Perhaps it was because of the stability. Perhaps it was because I wasn't at home with my family or at school with my friends. These were places where I didn't feel comfortable eating. I always felt like all eyes were on me. However, here at the hospital, no one was looking at me like I was crazy when I was eating. They all expected me to. And I knew I had to eat.

Slowly but surely, I was realizing how much energy food gave me. It physically made me feel better. I could also think more clearly. Aside from the constant feeling of fullness and the incessant constipation, eating became easier and easier. And because I didn't actually see my weight increasing in numbers, it didn't quite hit me that I was gaining weight. In the hospital, it was like I was hidden from reality. In fact, I was almost protected from it.

But as soon as I went home each day, the old thoughts and feelings would creep back into my mind. I automatically felt fat as soon as we turned into the driveway. And my desire to control something in my life took over the instant I walked in the door. Since I wasn't controlling my eating habits any longer, I turned to exercise as my new control mechanism.

Of course, it was healthy to exercise. But I was becoming so obsessed with exercising it had become harmful instead. I felt that if I missed just one night of sit-ups, my stomach would turn into blubber. I knew this wasn't rational, but I just couldn't stop. And just like that, since I wasn't controlling what I ate anymore, I had found a new obsession.

Diary Entry: 1/12/95

"...I really feel like I had a good day, although I would still like to exercise more and I don't enjoy eating. I am definitely scared that I won't eat when I leave the Carrier Program. Maybe it'll be easier if someone is there...it's the exercise I'm scared about. I can't stop. Hopefully, I'll learn how to stop. That's my goal for tomorrow.

Diary Entry: 1/18/95

I have been very tired lately but haven't been able to sleep. I also have been having horrible leg cramps. During group therapy today, we talked about being passive, assertive, and aggressive. I am certainly passive—I never speak up for myself. I guess I never realized it before and how unhealthy it can be, bottling up your emotions inside. I've realized a lot of my problems while I've been here. Hopefully, I'll be able to fix them when I get out of here. It's definitely been an experience.

We finally had a meeting today about returning to school. My treatment team decided that Monday would be the day. It's only five days away! I can't wait to see all of my friends. However, I am also hesitant to eat in front of everyone. They will all be looking at me! Well, I guess I am somehow going to have to get over that fear. I am now eating healthy, just like everybody else.

Unfortunately, I had a relapse tonight. I had decided to have a cup of lemon pudding as my snack. Mom made chocolate instead. The craving was overbearing since I hadn't had junk food in so long. I proceeded to eat ice cream, pretzels, and pieces of chocolate. I then felt so guilty about bingeing that I did two hours of exercise. Sit-ups, leg lifts...you name it. I just couldn't help myself. I felt like such a failure. Right now I feel so sick. Hopefully, I'll never eat like this again.

I mentioned this incident the next day in group therapy along with my other concerns, such as fears about going back to school. When admitting my binge at group, the first feeling I had was utter embarrassment. I was so ashamed that I had lost control. I didn't think any of the other patients would be able to understand. They had never talked about losing control with food. Only I lost control. Only I couldn't resist the evil temptations of junk food. Only I was a failure.

But after slowly and quietly admitting to what I had done, almost everyone else gave a sigh of relief. Following a slight pause, someone else admitted to doing the same thing a few nights prior. And then another patient had a similar experience to share. Pretty soon, just about everyone was able to share a time when they gave in to the temptations of food. "Whew!" I thought to myself. "I'm glad I wasn't the only one."

Everyone assured me that as long as I didn't deprive myself of all of the "bad" foods, I wouldn't feel as many urges to binge. If I could only allow myself to eat in moderation, then I would never need to plunge into every food at once. I couldn't believe that there was actually some logic behind that theory. It seemed to be true. The hard part would actually be believing it and then doing it. I just told myself, "Do what you have to do to be normal again." I didn't want to miss out on anything more.

My first day back at school eventually arrived. The hardest thing for me to face was eating lunch in the cafeteria with all of my friends. I asked one of my best friends, Maggie, to tell everyone else not to say anything about my new eating habits. These new behaviors, of course, included actually eating food as opposed to sucking on ice cubes. I knew it would be weird, and I was afraid that they would make a big deal out of it.

However, much to my surprise, when I arrived, no one said a thing. Their silence made everything even more awkward than I had imagined. It was like everyone was walking on eggshells around me. They didn't know what to say. I was extremely self-conscious.

I sat in my usual spot and opened my lunch bag. I had brought a bagel, an apple, and some skim milk, and amazingly, I ate mostly everything. I tried to chitchat and pretend like everything was normal, but it just felt so weird. I had been gone for so long but no one was asking about how I had been. On top of the awkward feelings, I physically felt like I wanted to explode. I hadn't eaten this much for lunch since elementary school. My hands were sweaty and I couldn't focus on a thing that anyone was saying. I just kept trying to make it through the conversation while anxiously awaiting the bell that would signal our next period.

Finally, the bell rang and I proceeded to my afternoon classes. Overall, the day was long, but I survived. I assumed it would get easier, just as my days got easier at the hospital. Once my friends got used to the idea that I was going to eat like the rest of them, I would feel better. And, more importantly, I had to get used to eating in front of them as well. This was certainly the bigger adjustment. For me, giving up my anorexia meant giving up my identity. For the first time since I could remember, I needed to focus on being me instead of being defined by my disease.

Don't give up. It's just the weight of the world.
When your heart's heavy, I will lift it for you.
Don't give up, because you want to be heard.
If silence keeps you, I will break it for you.
Everybody wants to be understood.
Well I can't hear you.
Everybody wants to be loved,
Don't give up, because you are loved.

–Josh Grobin, "You are Loved"

4 | rollercoaster ride

"One hundred and ten pounds? I can't believe I gained that much weight! I am so fat," I thought to myself after being weighed in. "I can't take it anymore. I need to go back to my old routine."

It had only been two weeks since I had left the outpatient program and I was already relapsing. The doctors had told me that relapsing a bit would be normal. The road to recovery was not a straight incline. It would be a bumpy road, but the further you got, the less bumpy it would be. It was hard to figure out where I was on this road to normalcy, but I was certainly at an extremely bumpy spot. There was no doubt about that.

I had started attending weekly group sessions back at the hospital with the other patients who had completed fulltime programs. The group therapy sessions met every Monday from seven p.m. to nine p.m. It was at these sessions that you were supposed to talk about the bumps in the road. I wanted to discuss the weight gain at the group meetings, but I didn't think that I'd get much support. Most of the women in the group were bulimic and were much older than me. I didn't feel like they could relate much, so I withheld my concerns at the next meeting. Nobody needed to know what I was really thinking about. I didn't even feel like coming to the group meetings anymore, to be perfectly honest. I just wanted to deal with my issues on my own.

Going back to school and being around my friends was very overwhelming. Trying to catch up on schoolwork was extremely intense. Being at home just gave me total anxiety. And on top of all of that came the fear surrounding food, which was overpowering as well. Essentially, nothing was easy that I was dealing with, especially since I was still trying to figure out the root cause of the eating disorder to begin with.

As a result, I decided to drop out of therapy. It was just too much to deal with in addition to everything else. I was hoping that I had learned enough to handle the rest of my issues on my own, and I wanted to heal at my own pace. Unforunately, one hundred and ten pounds was the trigger-mark for me. Everything was happening too quickly. I don't think I was ready to give up my identity just yet. I couldn't give it up because I didn't know what else to become.

Diary Entry: 2/5/95

I cannot believe how fat I am. I am so huge and flabby. I hate my body so much. That does it—I am going to lose at least 25 pounds. I think I want to weigh about 85 pounds. Then maybe I'll be happy. Just maybe. I've lost 4 pounds in the past week. 106 pounds is still pretty heavy. I don't understand how people can think that is skinny. I look and feel so huge. I want to be thin. I'll do anything!

Continuing to eat and be "normal" was a constant battle over the next few months, but I tried. I was keeping myself busy with practicing for my high school's spring musical, *Guys and Dolls*. And I had met a boy that I liked. He seemed to like me too, which was good. Dating was a good distraction for me. I had less time to isolate myself and think my negative thoughts. I kept myself occupied, which was the best solution.

Because of all the distractions, by the end of April, I had reluctantly developed a healthier outlook and routine. The boy that I had started dating made me realize that I was much more than a skinny blonde girl. Maybe there was more to life then just being thin. So I finally stopped weighing myself. I felt that if I looked okay, and if my clothes still fit, then the numbers on the scale didn't necessarily matter. But keeping this mentality wasn't easy. I had good days and bad days. Some days I felt fat, others I felt skinny. I still felt guilty about eating junk food, but at least I attempted to eat it on occasion. I didn't exercise as much. I felt better, looked better, and to my surprise, enjoyed life better.

Unfortunately, once I put a bathing suit on that May, my mind immediately changed.

Diary Entry: 5/14/95

Today, I laid outside in a two-piece bathing suit and I did not enjoy what I saw. I hate my body. I want to lose weight so badly. I'm so scared because I still want to be healthy. It's not fair. I think I need to start starving myself again but I'm not going to tell anyone. I can't afford to. They might send me back to Carrier, which didn't seem to help much. I need to be skinny. I am so messed up. If I'm not thin, then I don't want to live. Please, God, help me find a way. Nobody seems to help. Nobody seems to understand. Nobody seems to care. All I can do is cry.

Diary Entry: 5/19/95

I've started again. It's so depressing and disappointing. The past few days I started cutting back on what I've been eating by not eating breakfast. I pour a little cereal into a bowl with a little splash of milk and leave it on the counter. I'll also pour a little bit of juice into a glass and leave it there as well. This way it looks like I ate breakfast even though I didn't.

Today, I've been trying to make it all day without eating at all, knowing that I'll have to eat dinner with my parents. Meredith brought pretzels into the TV room after she ate lunch, and I was able to control myself when she offered me some. All I've had today is a glass of Diet Coke. I'm not even that hungry, surprisingly enough, but I do have a really bad headache. It stinks that I have to eat dinner, but I'm going to try to get away with as little as possible.

I miss the excitement from trying to deceive my parents and friends about eating. It's all about control. But I really hope it doesn't last this way forever. Just through the summer. Then I should be skinny and I'll be happy.

Diary Entry: 5/21/95

I bought diet pills today. I'm hoping they suppress my appetite. It makes starving myself so much easier. Today I only had a little dry cereal for breakfast and a tiny slice of pizza for dinner. The pizza was not by choice. I was with Mom. But that was it. Nothing more has entered my body and it feels great. I am back in control of what I'm eating and not eating. If I keep this up, I'll lose about ten pounds by the summer, perhaps twenty by summer's end. I'm even exercising again. It sort of feels good to be back to my old routine. I feel safe and comfortable. I missed the thrill of control. Obviously, I learned nothing when I was in the hospital. What a waste of time and money.

I was officially back to square one. I had told my mother in January that I would have to be at the "bottom of the barrel" before I could get better, and I honestly thought that I would never get any worse than how I was in January. But when I saw other patients that weighed eighty pounds or even less, I felt extremely jealous. I wanted to be as skinny as them. One hundred pounds wasn't bottom of the barrel for me. Obviously, things could get worse. Much worse.

So, unfortunately, I started the cycle once again. And this time, I was determined to get as skinny, if not skinnier, than the patients at the hospital. If they could do it, then I could do it. I just needed more discipline.

I had learned a few new tricks from the other patients at the hospital. I had gotten these ideas from the stories they would share during group therapy sessions. These habits were not shared, however, as positive experiences. They had discussed their problems with much negativity and fear. At the time, when I was on my way to a healthier place, I never imagined using these tricks as my own. I never thought I would be trying to lose weight again. But now that I was back to my old ways, I was determined to try anything that could help me lose weight, even if they weren't healthy behaviors.

The first were laxatives. I took them whenever I ate. I assumed that since the food came out of me so quickly that not many calories were being absorbed. In my mind, it was like throwing up in a different sort of way. I desperately wanted to believe this theory. Psychologically, it made sense. However, I had learned the calories were absorbed just the same, with or without the laxatives. Of course, I didn't care. I still felt better knowing the food was leaving my body quicker than it normally would. I couldn't stand to have food in my body. It felt so disgusting. I felt much prettier without food inside me. I felt lighter and cleaner and empty. Empty was good. No food. No emotion. Just empty.

That summer, I worked at the local day camp. Every day I told my mother that I was going to buy lunch along with the other counselors, but instead I'd watch my twenty-seven happy campers eat their lunches while I ate nothing. When they asked where my lunch was, I always told them that the camp counselors ate inside at a different time. None of them would ever question me, so I just assumed that they believed me. And luckily, none of the other counselors ever questioned me about my lack of lunch either. Full days out in the sun without food were tough, but I made it through. I had to. I just had to get skinny.

Diary Entry: 7/9/95

Well, I've lost weight. Yeah! But unfortunately, I am so constipated right now. I haven't gone to the bathroom in thirteen days. I went away for the weekend with my boyfriend and couldn't take laxatives. Now, finally, I can again, and I'm still waiting for them to work their magic. I feel so sick.

It's a shame that I never got better, but I can't seem to give up that sense of control. Sometimes I binge because I go for such long periods of depriving myself. Then I get into social situations where I have to eat and have no excuse. But once I start eating, it's hard to stop and then afterwards, I feel like such a failure.

I know I need help again, but I don't want it. Part of me likes being sick. I just hope I don't ruin my life forever. Sometimes I get so down, all I can do is cry. I can't figure out why, but I get in these moods where I just want to crawl up into a ball, be all alone, and cry. I feel so unloved, but at the same time I feel smothered by everyone. I feel smothered by my parents. When I'm at home, I feel like I have no space. At every moment, suggestions about how to live my life are thrown at me. I feel like the only way to escape is to turn myself off from everyone. Isolate myself. Be alone and think. And this is what I do. Whether I'm at home, at school, or at a party, I just turn myself off like a light switch. For some reason, I'm searching for someone or something that can give me permission to be myself. I want to feel comfortable being myself, and I want to feel comfortable expressing my own opinions and making my own decisions. But for some reason, I just can't feel these things.

"Jen, you have a phone call," my junior counselor screamed across the soccer field. "I think it's your sister."

It was another typical day at camp. I casually strolled across the field into the main office where the tan 1970s-style touch-tone phone rested atop the gray metal desk.

"Hello?...Hey Mer, what's up?...She did what?...How could she?...She's on her way here now?...Are you kidding?... I can't believe that she is doing this!" I desperately shouted.

Luckily, no one else was in the office. "I gotta go. I think I see her car now. Thanks for the warning…I'll see you at home. Bye," I muttered.

I could not believe what I had just heard. My mother was on her way over to bring me lunch. She had gone through my room and read my diary. She knew absolutely everything! She knew all about my eating habits, my eating rituals, and my secrets. She knew all about the laxatives and diet pills. Heck, she probably found those too and threw them out! What was I going to do? What would I say? I felt so betrayed. My stomach was in my throat.

I didn't have much time to collect my thoughts because she had just pulled up and was getting out of her old Buick station wagon. She stormed right over to me and practically threw a brown paper lunch bag at me.

"Here," she shouted. "Please eat this. You need the energy. You're going to fall over and pass out. Please, just eat it." Luckily, no one was around, so we could speak freely in the middle of the camp parking lot.

"Mom, how could you do this to me? How could you invade my privacy like this?" I asked. "I'm trying. I really am," I exclaimed in desperation. "I'm just confused. I'm fine, really, I'm fine. Just leave me alone. Just leave."

She looked at me with disappointment as the tears streamed down her face. I knew she was frustrated and scared. I was too. But she had nothing more to say. I don't think she knew what to say. She just shook her head and walked back to her car. I remained in the parking lot, grasping the brown paper bag as tight as I could. I knew she only did what she did because she loved me. But that didn't mean it was right.

As she walked away, my mixed emotions began to rise to the surface. Hurt, anger, frustration, sadness. I had lost all the trust I had in my mother. I couldn't understand how she could do this to me. My diary was the one place where I could be completely honest. It was the one place where I felt safe enough to divulge my greatest secrets or biggest fears. There was no one to judge me. There was no one that could tell me I was wrong for having the feelings that I had. I could be honest. And I could try to eventually make sense of it all.

But now my privacy was gone. My safe place had disappeared. What was I going to do? All I wanted to do was run after her and scream, "How could you do this to me?" But I couldn't. I was now surrounded by hundreds of little kids and counselors, and she had driven off towards the main street.

As soon as I got home, I approached my mother, who was out back watering her impatiens. I decided that it was time to let some of my anger out. And not just because of the invasion of privacy. There were feelings of anger that had been building up for some time. Once I began, it was hard to stop. I couldn't stop screaming or crying for hours. It felt so good to be angry and to finally release some of my pent-up feelings.

I had felt so betrayed—and by my own mother nonetheless. I couldn't even fathom the vast amount of knowledge she had now acquired from reading my notes. She now knew all of my secrets. She would never believe my lies or promises ever again. I had to convince her that I was trying to get better and there was only one thing left to do. Write fake journal entries.

Diary Entry: 7/11/95

Yesterday, my mother went through my room and read this diary. I feel so violated! Now she can't trust me anymore when it comes to eating. I'll just have to gain her trust back but the only way to do that is to get better. It's certainly going to be tough but I think I can do it. I definitely want to do it. As long as I can stick with eating healthy foods, then I won't feel as guilty. Then she won't have to worry anymore and everything can go back to normal.

Of course, this journal entry was a bunch of bullshit. I only wrote it in case my mother found my diary and read it again. This way, she would think that I was honestly trying to get better. I even left the diary out on purpose so she would find it and read it. Needless to say, I thought I was pretty clever.

Diary Entry: 8/20/95

Okay, I'm not getting any better. Over the past month, I've become the worst I've ever been. I hardly eat at all—only in front of people so they will think I'm okay. And if and when I do eat, I take at least three laxatives. Sometimes I lose control and binge on everything in sight: ice cream, cookies, Pringles, Rice Krispy Treats, etc. and then I get really depressed, sometimes even suicidal. I come upstairs to my bedroom and take at least twenty laxatives. Occasionally, I go into the shower and cut myself purposely with a razor in places where people won't see (like my stomach, the tops of my feet, the back of my neck, or the tops of my thighs). This is my way to punish myself for being "bad." I see my skin splitting, and watch the blood mix with the water as it slowly flows into the drain. I feel pain but somehow feel peace at the same time.

Eating was bad, I kept telling myself. For some reason, everyone else was allowed to eat, but I wasn't. I had to punish myself over and over again. I strangely enjoyed it. I enjoyed feeling the pain. Actually, I guess I just enjoyed feeling anything in general, even if it was physical agony.

It had been so long since I had felt anything whether it be happiness, sadness, or anger. I had conditioned myself to push my feelings down inside, down so far I didn't even know they existed. I would always put on a happy face even if I was having a bad day. For some reason, I had to be the strong one. I had to be happy. I don't know why I had to be this way. It just felt right.

Perhaps I didn't want my parents to know that I was upset about their relationship. Perhaps I didn't want my friends to know that I didn't feel like I fit in. I didn't want anyone to acknowledge my feelings. I kept them bottled up inside of me, like a bottle out at sea. No one to hear, no one to see. Just an empty bottle floating aimlessly with no real direction or purpose.

Diary Entry: 8/21/95

I'm scared. I'm scared because I have scars all over my body. I'm scared because my hair is coming out. I'm cold all of the time, my stomach hurts constantly, I haven't had my period in a few months, and I've had four leg cramps over the past five days. I also cannot concentrate at all. I hardly have any energy. And, on top of all that, I look and feel so fat! I hate myself so much!

Diary Entry: 8/29/95

All I want to do is lock myself in my room away from everyone and from food until I look totally emaciated. I'm starting to get large bruises on the back of my right hand from sticking my hand down my throat every time I accidentally binge on food. I guess I'm starting to bruise pretty easily.

Also, because of the laxatives (I'm assuming), I now go to the bathroom unconsciously. I peed once when I was babysitting and once last night at the movies. I didn't even notice until after I got up and realized my pants were wet. It is so embarrassing. But unfortunately, it is not enough to scare me to stop this cycle of self-mutilation. All I've done all morning is cry. I need someone who can understand me, since I don't even understand myself. I only weigh 110 but want to weigh less. I recently started playing soccer, so I'm sure that will help.

The last few weeks of summer were consistent, which was helpful. Being on a set schedule made it easier for me to figure out my eating routine. I would get to soccer practice around nine a.m. without having eaten breakfast. We would do circuit training in the morning: mostly running around the track and doing pushups in between. I would get so exhausted that I would fake a hamstring pull in order to rest. Around noon, we would then have an hour break for lunch.

Instead of hanging out with the rest of my teammates to eat, I drove to our town's local park to be alone. I would actually throw out the lunches that my mother had given me, and instead of eating I'd read a book and drink soda. Around one o'clock, I would return to the field to practice foot and field work. This lasted until around three thirty. As anyone could imagine, by the time I would get home, I would be physically exhausted. I would take a nap until dinner and then try to weasel out of it. I would either make up a story about meeting someone that night or I would tell my parents that I didn't feel comfortable at the dinner table and needed to eat alone. Much to my surprise, it usually worked.

I'd go out for a few hours, whether it was to meet up with my boyfriend or friends. And of course, if they were eating, I'd make up a story that I had already eaten dinner. I'd finally return to my house, try to exercise more before going to bed, eventually fall asleep after hours of tossing and turning, and then wake up around eight a.m. to start the cycle all over again.

Diary Entry: 8/31/95

I can't believe how bad it has gotten. When I eat a mint, or even have just a sip of something other than diet soda or water, I feel like I binged. And lately, since Mom knows that I haven't been doing too well, we have been getting into many fights. Most recently she threatened to take away my car, withdraw me from the soccer program, and cancel my dance lessons. It's sad to say, but none of these things that used to make me happy matter as much as losing weight. During one argument, I told her that, and that nothing she or anyone else could do would help me. I don't want to be helped. Meredith stood on the sidelines, crying as we screamed back and forth, and it didn't affect me one bit.

My boyfriend was a year older than me, and he was leaving for college the week before my senior year of high school began.

I decided I wanted to cook him dinner and have him over with my entire family before he left. I made an extensive three course meal, including a decadent chocolate cake for dessert. I tried eating as little as possible that night, even a little of the chocolate cake. I couldn't resist. It tasted so good. I hadn't had chocolate in so long. Throughout the rest of the night, I couldn't stop thinking about it. I wanted more but couldn't have any in front of anyone. I couldn't let them see me during a moment of weakness. I'd have to wait until everyone was asleep.

My boyfriend finally left around eleven thirty p.m. My mom and sister were already in bed asleep, and my dad was downstairs in the basement, passed out in front of the television. I went upstairs, pretending to go to bed, and waited about an hour before I came back down. I tried to talk myself out of the binge because I knew how badly I'd feel afterwards, but I couldn't resist. My mind was made up. I needed to have that cake.

I crept down the stairs and was sure everyone was still asleep. I quietly snuck into the kitchen and took the cake out of the refrigerator. I couldn't wait. I cut a tiny sliver, finished it off, and immediately decided that I wanted more. I wanted the entire cake and probably would have finished it too if my mother hadn't caught me.

"Jennifer, control yourself!" she screamed, as she appeared from the hallway. She hustled over as fast as she could and tried to grab the cake from me, but I wouldn't let go. I was on a mission.

I had nothing to say. I was caught, red-handed and there was no way I could talk myself out of this situation. So I continued to stay focused on the cake, as I was already in the binge zone which wasn't easy to escape.

Before she could jostle it away from me, I dove my hands into the plate to get as much cake as possible. Tears were streaming down my face as she screamed, "You need help, Jennifer. You are so sick! Do you know that? You need help!"

"I know," I cried, gasping for air, "I know!"

As soon as the fistfuls of cake were in my mouth I ran upstairs into the bathroom, slammed the door, and slid down the side of the wall while I licked the excess cake off my hands. It still tasted good.

Meanwhile, my mother threw out the rest of the cake and cleaned up the kitchen. Eventually, I got up and stared into the mirror to find a face covered with chocolate cake and hair matted with vanilla icing. I began to rinse off my hands and arms while I gazed into my red swollen eyes. I felt so ashamed. I felt so helpless. I felt like a completely different person, as if I was acting out a scene from a TV movie. "Who acts like this?" I thought to myself. This isn't normal.

I finally got myself all cleaned up and brought a warm wet washcloth into my room. I slowly closed my bedroom door, placed the warm washcloth over my swollen eyes, and went to bed. The chocolate cake incident was never mentioned again.

Diary Entry: 9/25/95

I really hope that this isn't my last entry. I've done something stupid and unthinkable. I don't know why, but I get these uncontrollable urges to eat, even if I'm not hungry. Tonight, I binged on an apple, grapes, a pear, and a ton of crackers with peanut butter spread on top of them. Afterwards, I felt so depressed and disgusted with myself. I was so disappointed that I had lost control. I began to realize that I didn't want to live like this anymore. But I don't want help because I don't want to get fat. I just want to stop bingeing. And if I can't, then I don't want to live anymore. I took four laxatives, but I knew that wouldn't satisfy me. That wasn't enough punishment, so I took ten Cephalexin capsules. I don't want to die, I just want to escape from all my feelings and sleep for a very long time. Hopefully, I've accomplished this goal by taking these pills. We will see.

Diary Entry: 9/26/95

Luckily, everything was fine. I laid in bed today and slept all day into the next. I told no one about this, and luckily my mom never thought to ask.

I was really pushing my limits now. I was doing things to my body that were unheard of, extreme things in order to gain attention. But why? Why did I desire this negative attention so badly? My journal writing was helping me analyze my actions and examine my upbringing.

Maybe my mother's low self-esteem had set a pattern that I felt I was supposed to follow. Maybe I couldn't see all of my great accomplishments because she couldn't see hers.

Or maybe I was trying to get attention from my father. He was a workaholic who spent all of his free time down in the basement watching TV.

I needed to figure out the reason that was driving my eating disorder addiction. It was the only way I could resolve the pattern. Once I was able to deal with the issues, I wouldn't rely on the eating disorder as my vice.

It was the same as any addiction, really, the same as it is for an alcoholic or drug addict. Some people drink for the diversion. It becomes their escape from reality, and they become reliant on alcohol as the solution to their problems. They may try to quit cold turkey. They may try to convince themselves that they will stop drinking all on their own. But how can they do that if they don't know what the root cause of the issue is to begin with?

I could promise myself that I wouldn't starve anymore, but eating was so hard. I didn't have an appetite, and I couldn't bring myself to eat when my stomach wasn't asking for food. When I could make it a few days without a binge, I'd get a natural high from the control. And then my promises would go right out the window.

Starving had become what I lived for, feeling the rush of accomplishment that I felt throughout my body whenever I went a whole day without eating a thing. I would live on Diet Coke and maybe a stick of gum here and there. I believed that the caffeine from the soda would take me through the day and that was all that I needed.

My senior year had finally come. This year would be a year to remember. It was my last year of high school. This should have been a positive time in my life. I had freedom. I had my driver's license. I had great friends. I had a shorter class schedule which meant even more free time. My life should have been worry-free.

But somehow, all I could focus on was the negative. Yes, I may have had all of these wonderfully positive things in my life, but the most important of all my concerns was that I wasn't skinny enough. All I cared about was getting as skinny as possible.

I needed to be the best at something. I needed it. I wanted it. And if being skinny was it, then so be it. I wanted everyone to look at me and be jealous.

At the beginning of the school year, I started making up stories about when and how much I would eat. I was officially back to my old ways. On the first day, I found out my class schedule, realizing that I only had one class after lunch and then was able to go home. This worked out perfectly.

I came up with a plan to tell everyone that I ate a large breakfast in the morning before school and then would eat lunch when I got home. I explained to my closest friends that I still didn't quite feel comfortable with eating in front of everyone and that I felt more relaxed at home. This was the perfect excuse.

I sipped a Diet Coke every day at the lunch table while everyone else ate their normal lunches, and after school I made sure to keep myself occupied at all times. I'd also make certain every night I had plans so I could have some type of excuse to get out of eating dinner. In the fall there were yearbook meetings, dance classes, soccer games, and tutoring sessions, not to mention the time I spent with my friends. So normally I was never home at dinnertime, which worked out perfectly. I could go for days without having to eat a full meal.

However, the weekends were a lot more difficult, especially when I had a bunch of free time. Not only could I not get out of meals, but I would sometimes cave in to my hunger all on my own and eat without being forced. Starving myself made me think about food even more, and sometimes I'd get to a point where I just ate everything in sight. Bingeing became my new bad habit and vice.

Bingeing was like an out-of-body experience. I'd try to go as long as I could without eating anything of high caloric value, but eventually I'd hit a breaking point. Sooner or later, I would talk myself into buying all of my forbidden foods and eat them all at once. About a month after the chocolate cake incident, I slipped again, but this time in complete secrecy.

It was a typical Saturday morning, my sister and I both lounging around in the tv room watching Star Search. I couldn't focus on the tv, however, since all I could think about was food. "Should I binge or should I remain strong?" I thought to myself. I so desperately wanted to stay strong but at the same time, I needed to eat. I couldn't fast any longer. If I binged, I could take a bunch of laxatives which would empty me out in no time. "It'd be worth it," I concluded. And so my mind was set. I was going to binge.

Before I could change my mind, I changed into jeans and a tee-shirt and ran to the grocery store where I bought everything from cookies and cupcakes to candy and ice cream. Sweets were what I was craving.

Before I returned from the store, I had put all the food into a duffle bag so I could smuggle it upstairs into my bedroom.

Once I got to my room, I closed my door, took everything out, and lined it up on the floor. The blue Rice Krispy Treat box was the most tempting, so that was first. I figured I would let the ice cream melt a little bit, so I decided to make that last. The cupcakes, cookies, Sun Chips and Pringles were lined up inbetween and I was finally ready to begin.

I opened my first Rice Krispy Treat and then immediately scrounged for the next item to eat. While stuffing the last of the marshmallow treat in my mouth, I desperately tried to open the plastic container, which held the freshly made cupcakes. I proceeded to stuff an entire cupcake in my mouth, all at once. It tasted so good. I couldn't remember the last time I had eaten chocolate. I had to lick every last crumb off my lips before I could divulge in the Pepperidge Farms cookies that I had bought. After eating a few cookies, I then tried to engulf some sour cream and onion Pringles potato chips, but my stomach was already feeling full.

I saw the bag of Sun Chips and the half-gallon of mint chocolate chip ice cream staring back at me but at this point, couldn't fathom eating any of it. I was so full but at the same time, I desperately wanted to finish everything in sight. I just wanted to put it all in my mouth so I didn't have to look at it anymore. As I stuffed a fourth potato chip in my mouth, I began to realize that I didn't even taste it anymore. I couldn't taste anything. It all seemed bland.

I couldn't force one more bite down my throat, but I looked around and still saw a lot of food. What was I going to do with it? I had to get rid of it somehow. I threw it all in my soccer bag and hid it in the closet. As soon as I threw the bag in the closet and closed the doors, I sat back in the middle of my bedroom floor. Silence. Although the radio was blasting, I heard nothing but silence. I felt empty and numb. What had I just done?

Seconds later, I realized how uncomfortable my stomach felt. Now all I wanted to do was vacuum out my insides. But how? I needed to throw up. I needed to get rid of everything inside. But I couldn't make myself get sick. I had tried so many times before. I just had to wait it out and try the alternative which would be to take an entire box of laxatives and go to bed. I just wanted it all to go away. I wanted to fall into a deep sleep and wake up from this horrible nightmare and have it be completely overwith.

I felt sick for days after this incident. Binges never made me feel good. I would only experience a few moments of euphoria, a few magical moments when I wasn't counting calories. But then I'd have to deal with the aftermath, the physical discomfort of the bloated stomach and the psychological trauma from consuming massive amounts of calories. I would literally beat myself up after a binge. I had failed myself. I had given in to my desires and eaten food, which I was not allowed to do.

After this specific binge, I decided to make a promise to myself in written form. A promise that bonded together all of my beliefs and plans that had to do with starvation and loosing weight. This promise letter, although short and to the point, could have very well been a legal document, as I signed it at the bottom in order to remind myself of the seriousness of my goal. My goal to become as skinny as possible without dying.

I carried this signed document around with me, everywhere I went. And whenever I got the urge to eat, I took out this letter and read it to myself.

Letter: 9/29/95

Right now, I am going to make a commitment to myself. It is 9/29/95, at 9:36 p.m. My goal is to lose weight. I don't know how much. I would like to get into the eighties, around eighty-five pounds would be nice. Whenever I want to binge, I will think of this goal. Even if I lose it once, may it be for others or myself, it does not make it right to keep bingeing. I must lose weight—I have to. There is nothing else I can control. I know how horrible I feel after I eat a lot.

Let me remember this when I get the urge. I hope this works. No more bingeing! I don't want to get fat.

Jennifer Otto
P.S. Chew gum!

Diary Entry: 10/16/95

I need to make this commitment to myself right now. No more bingeing. I am going to lose weight and be happy! ☺

Diary Entry: 11/4/95

I am so excited! I just found a new way to control my bingeing problem. I read in a magazine article that there is this medicine that is sold in drug stores that induces vomiting. Now, I'll be able to binge and get rid of it all very easily. The only problem is that this liquid medicine is only allowed to be sold to people who are over eighteen years old. Hopefully, I'll get around that issue.

I just got back from the drug store. They didn't ask any questions. I just told them what I needed and they got it for me. It was really cheap, too! This is going to make things a whole lot easier. They say this stuff isn't that good for you. It can cause permanent heart problems and stuff like that. But it shouldn't be a problem for me. I'm not going to be using it every day or anything. I should be fine.

Diary Entry: 1/1/96

It is two thirty a.m. The new year has just begun. This is the day to make my resolutions. Well, the one and only one which is of most importance to me is as follows: food makes me sick. Therefore, starting today, I will not eat anything. Only liquids may pass my lips. I must get skinny. I currently weigh ninety-four pounds. I am way too fat!

Monday morning came and went, filled with frivolous conversation about our music teacher's surprise baby shower. I was greatly looking forward to it. I just loved surprises. We had all planned to bring different foods for the event, mostly desserts, since it was to be held in one of the classrooms that night after choir practice.

Once practice was over, we scrambled to the classroom in order to finish preparations and await her arrival. Once she made it and the surprising was over with, we were all able to relax and peruse the surplus of delectable treats.

I had planned to forego the food as usual. But once I saw the Rice Krispy Treats and mint chocolate bars, along with all the chips and dip, I started to convince myself to binge. While everyone else around me gossiped and visited, I was having a conversation with myself inside my head, trying to decide whether to indulge in the evil foods or not. I just couldn't decide.

Should I eat? Or should I stay in control? I did have the vomit-inducing medicine at home, so if I did eat, I'd be able to get rid of it once I got home. How often did I have the opportunity to have fresh-baked cookies or cake? Not very. That did it. I had convinced myself I would eat. But now I had to get away with it inconspicuously. No one was used to seeing me eat to begin with, so if I was going to binge, I had to do it under the radar.

I started at one end of the room where the mint brownies were. I picked up one along with a Rice Krispy Treat and stuffed both in my mouth really quickly before anyone could see. I then put the plate down and went to have a conversation with my friend Evan. He was talking to me and I tried to listen, but all I could think about was how good the food had just tasted and what I was going to eat next. I politely nodded as he rambled on and on. I finally decided that I was ready for some chips. So at that point, I curtly ended our conversation so I could move over to the other side of the room to grab some additional munchies.

On the way over to the other side of the room, I grabbed a few cookies and a small piece of cake. Again, I ate them as quickly as possible so nobody saw how much I was eating. I then grabbed some chips and hummus on my plate while I chatted with my friend Natalie. Again, she spoke while I had my own conversation going on inside my head. I didn't hear a word she was saying. I just kept on nodding while figuring out how much more I could eat before someone noticed I was bingeing.

When I finally decided to leave, I grabbed a napkin with a few black and white cookies and another mint brownie. Those things were phenomenal. I snuck out the door without saying goodbye to anyone. I wanted to be able to walk to my car alone while I finished my cookies and brownie. Although I had started to feel sick and my stomach was about to explode, the desserts still tasted wonderful. I knew in about thirty minutes they'd all be gone and my stomach would feel as good as new. I just needed to get home.

I drove as fast as I could. Five minutes later I reached my house, where I had barely pulled into the driveway when I opened the door, turned the key, and ran inside. I frantically ran up stairs without even saying hello to my family and rushed right towards my bedside table for the magical liquid. The toxic medication would bring all of the "bad" foods right out of my system.

Since I had taken this medication many times before, one tablespoon wouldn't work anymore. My body had grown immune to it. I now had to drink the entire bottle of toxic stuff in order to obtain any results. I somehow managed to drink the entire bottle, and then I got ready for bed while waiting for the toxin to take effect.

About twenty minutes later, I felt an unstoppable urge to throw up. I quietly ran into the bathroom. Three minutes later, everything, including the first brownie I ate, was out of my system and in the toilet. "What a relief!" I thought to myself.

I felt so much better. Aside from the constant burning sensation and gritty feeling in my throat, I felt fine. I was able to ignore the acidic feeling throughout my entire body. All I cared about was that my stomach was now empty. It went from being a huge bubble to an empty pit. And it was all because of this ingenious medication.

Days went by. It had gotten to the point where I just stared at the clock waiting for time to pass. The more time that went by without eating the more weight I lost, so I just wanted the clock to keep ticking away. Tick…tick…tick…I couldn't concentrate on anything. When I was in class, I counted calories in the margin of my notebook.

Stick of gum: ten calories. Fat-free hot chocolate: forty calories. Total: fifty calories. Ugh, ten more than yesterday. I'm going to have to cut back.

Each day was in competition with the last, to see if I could take in fewer calories. Some days I obtained that goal. Other days I did not. When I was pleased with my intake for the day, I was deliriously happy. On the days where I was disappointed in myself, I couldn't even bear the thought of talking to another soul. On those days, I just wanted to crawl up into a ball and cry. And I usually ended up doing this. All day long. I honestly thought the reason I was crying was because of my lack of control. At the time, I could never imagine that it might be because of my parent's relationship or my lack of self-esteem.

It was now February, and at this point, a binge was considered a piece of pizza or a french fry. My major decisions of each day consisted of whether or not I should allow myself to eat a Blow-Pop (calories=60). If I did allow myself a Blow-Pop, I made sure that I did enough physical activity that day in order to burn off the extra calories.

I was falling into a whirlpool of obsessive thoughts, none of which I could control. Some days I wanted to stay in the pool, others I tried helplessly to get out. My eating disorder was now in control, and I was completely out of the driver's seat. And somewhere inside, I knew that I was. But I felt that I would never be happy unless I was the skinniest person alive. That would show that I had the most control over anyone. I now weighed eighty-nine pounds and looked very much like a young girl prior to hitting puberty. Which was just perfect for playing the part of an orphan in our upcoming Spring musical, *Little Orphan Annie.*

Play practice started at nine a.m. Saturday morning. I packed my backpack with my clothes for dress rehearsal, along with a lukewarm Diet Sprite for my mid-day's meal. Throughout the day I reminded myself to sip the diet soda in moderation, since it had to last through the ten-hour rehearsal day. By three o'clock, I was extremely fatigued and could barely see straight. I began viewing everything as if it were through a black piece of paper with a hole in the middle. It was like I had tunnel vision and couldn't focus on anything in sight.

"Jen, c'mon, we gotta go change for the run-through," Katie informed me as I sat staring into space. I reluctantly grabbed my bag and followed her and a few others into the ladies' room.

Anxiety quickly sank in. All of the stalls were taken, and I had no choice but to change in the middle of the bathroom in front of the other girls. Part of me felt so fat and ugly. But another part of me, deep down inside, knew how skinny I really was. At eighty-nine pounds with my ribcage sticking out, I knew that I did not look normal. Either way, I had no choice. I took a deep breath and told myself to just pretend like nothing was wrong. "Chat with everyone else and act normal," I thought.

And with that, I slowly took off my pants, allowing my long T-shirt to cover most of my body. I stepped into the size 12 dress (a children's 12, I might add) and brought it up to rest on my hipbones. I then took my arms out of my T-shirt and tried to put each arm into the sleeves of the dress while keeping the T-shirt hovering over me like a tent. Unfortunately, it would not cooperate.

Once I had my arms into the sleeves, I had to take the T-shirt off in order to get my shoulders and the rest of my body into the dress successfully. So there I stood, with a full-on view of my bony collarbones and ribcage. I caught a quick glimpse in the mirror, and couldn't believe how disgusting I looked.

I quickly finished putting on the dress while keeping up the conversation, and casually asked Katie to zip up my dress. Fortunately, no one said anything, and all I could hope was that no one really noticed or cared. I wanted so badly to keep losing weight, and I wasn't about to let anything or anyone stop me.

A few days later came opening night of our high school production. Thursday, Friday, and Saturday were three exciting nights of performing and partying. Each night, after our performance, we would all head over to someone's house to celebrate our big success.

Thursday night I controlled myself rather well. I denied all offers for food. "Jen, do you want a slice of pizza?" someone would ask. "No thanks," I would reply. I didn't need the extra calories. "I had a large dinner to give me extra energy for the big performance," I said. Well, not exactly. I had about two cans of Diet Coke before each show and that was about it.

I controlled myself on Friday night as well. No food passed my lips and I was extremely impressed with myself. But then came Saturday, the last night of our big performance. As soon as the show ended, the entire cast ventured over to a local restaurant that had been rented out for us. I arrived and sat with a bunch of my closest friends in one of the restaurant booths. As usual, I had no plans of eating anything or drinking anything for that matter.

But everyone began swarming towards the tower of pizza boxes and extra-large sheet cake. After only five minutes of usual subconscious debate, I gave in to the battle. "Just have one piece. One piece won't hurt you. You're skinny enough to afford one piece of pizza. Don't worry about it. Everyone else is allowing themselves to have multiple pieces. Just join in," I thought to myself.

"What? Are you crazy? You can't have a piece. That would be out of control. That would be giving in to your desire. You can't quit now. That would be like surrendering. You can't give up. You can do it. Just concentrate on the conversation, not what they are eating," I then rebutted in my mind.

But I couldn't. I had to have just one piece. One small, tiny piece of pizza. Just then, my friend was going up for seconds and asked if I wanted to go with him. "Sure," I said. "I'm starving." And I was. Literally.

I finally felt like one of the gang. For the first time in a long time, I was eating with my friends. I felt normal for the first time in over a year. And, to my surprise, no one said a word about me eating pizza.

It was such a good feeling that I decided to take advantage of the situation. After eating one slice of pizza, I went back to take a piece of cake! I couldn't believe it. I was completely out of control, as this was now turning into a binge.

Once I finished the cake, all I could think about was going home to use the vomit-inducer that would get rid of all the food and calories that had just entered my body. My little bottle of magic liquid was waiting for me in my nightstand. The answer to all of my problems was jammed inside that little bottle. That liquid would be able to take away all of the pain. Once I could get home to that bottle, all of my guilt would go away and everything would be back to status quo.

Once I got home, I drank the toxin and waited for the results. The results came up, and I automatically felt better. Although I still felt guilty about losing control, I had some peace of mind that most of the calories were out of my system. Once again, I vowed to myself that I would never ever lose control like that again. I would never give in to my temptations. I had to be different. I had to lose weight. I had to get skinny. But most importantly, I had to stay in control.

Diary Entry: 2/19/96

I hate this disease so much. I wish I could magically make it disappear. It has ruined my life. It ruined my relationships with friends, relatives, and most importantly, myself. I absolutely hate myself. And I hate everyone trying to help me. I don't want help. I now weigh 89 pounds. I thought this would be my goal weight. But I've realized that one number is never going to be enough. I might as well weigh 289 pounds because I feel that fat. All I want to do is be skinny, love myself, and love life. But I can't see this ever happening all at the same time. I know I have to choose one or the other, but it's too hard. It's like a war going on in my head. And both sides are losing.

And then a hero comes along
With the strength to carry on
And you cast your fears aside
And you know you can survive
So when you feel like hope is gone
Look inside you and be strong
And you'll finally see the truth
That a hero lies in you

–Mariah Carey, "Hero"

5 | safe haven

Winter break should have been a time of relaxation and enjoyment. I had been working extremely hard during my senior year in order to prepare for college. Thus, I was greatly looking forward to the opportunity to relax and spend some time with my friends.

Unfortunately, every night my friends made plans which usually included some type of meal. And without fail, every night I would come up with some excuse as to why I couldn't meet them for dinner but would be able to meet up with them after. But by Tuesday, the fourth day of my vacation, my days of relaxation and excuse-making were over.

Tuesday morning was typical. I woke up around eight a.m. After doing some exercises alone in my room I showered, got dressed, and dried my hair. Maggie and I had plans to go to the Livingston Mall that afternoon.

Shortly after getting ready, I went downstairs, popped open a can of Diet Orange Slice, and flipped on the TV. I sat on the couch immersed in the last five minutes of *Regis and Kathy Lee* when my mother's friend, Mrs. Zaba, rang the doorbell. Mrs. Zaba was not only my mother's closest friend, but she was also the mother of one of my best friends. It was unusual for her to be stopping by since my mother wasn't home. Needless to say, I was a bit puzzled.

With reservation, I slowly opened the front door to find Mrs. Zaba standing on our front porch wearing an old black sweat suit, with her unwashed curly hair pulled back in a ponytail. She did not look happy.

"Hi Jen, can I come in?" she meekly asked.

"Sure," I hesitantly replied. I knew this couldn't be good.

As she stepped into our living room, she casually wiped a tear off her cheek and made her way into the kitchen. "Your mom and I are very worried about you, Jen," she firmly stated. "We really want you to get some help." The tears began to flow as she continued to lecture me on how beautiful and talented I was and how I was ruining my entire life by starving myself.

"I know I need more help, Mrs. Zaba," I reluctantly agreed. "I'm working hard to get better. I just need to do this on my own and in my own time. I can't be forced into getting better. I have to truly want it."

Well, she disagreed. She stared at me with desperation while she began to matter-of-factly inform me that I was going to be taken to the hospital that afternoon. Of course, I wanted to scream at her. I wanted to tell her that I wasn't going to go. But I couldn't scream at my friend's mother. She was only trying to help. What I needed was to scream at my own mother. And I soon had the opportunity.

As if on cue, my mother showed up within minutes of our conversation. She had taken a half-day off work so she could bring me to the hospital. She walked in, and I immediately turned down the offer.

"Mom, I'm not going. I know you both want me to get help, but I'm not going to get better unless you leave me alone. I'm not going to get better unless I want to get better," I stated.

I had a feeling that wasn't going to work, but I knew I just needed to try.

Within two minutes, my father showed up as well. He, too, had taken a half-day off work in order to bring me to the hospital. This was the first time I had ever seen my mother and father work together on something. Usually they worked as separate parties, never as a team.

Perhaps this was why I had gone through all of this. Perhaps it was an unconscious effort to make my parents talk to each other. Who knows? All I knew was that I was in the process of being shipped off to some institution without my own consent. I was still under eighteen, so my parents had full control over the situation. I felt helpless.

"Run up to your room and grab what you want to take with you," my mother recommended. "We already have a bag of clothes for you, but if there's something specific we've missed, this is your last chance." If Mrs. Zaba wasn't there, I would have been more reluctant. I probably would have even driven away in my own car. But because she was there, I had to act mature. I had to handle the situation with as much dignity and control as possible. But being forced into a car wasn't what I had in mind.

So with a childish sulk on my face, I stormed out of the house and into the family station wagon. We were officially on our way to the hospital. I just hoped they weren't going to make me eat. "Please God, don't let them feed me," I thought.

The ride to the hospital was complete agony. Everyone was silent: Dad driving, Mom in the passenger seat, and me sitting in the back seat, staring out the window wondering what was about to happen. I tried my hardest to figure out an alternative but the only thing I could come up with was jumping out of the car and running for my life. The only issue with this option was that I wasn't sure where I would go if I was actually successful.

I had even read an article in Teen magazine that talked about a girl who had been in the same situation. Her parents threw her in a car and started driving her to a hospital, where she was supposed to stay to get help with her eating disorder. She actually did jump out of the car on the way to the hospital but unfortunately, she died almost instantly. But she didn't die from getting hit by a car, or even the impact from the fall. She died because her heart stopped from the shock. That story ran through my mind as I was contemplating the idea. At that moment, I decided that committing suicide just wasn't the answer. I didn't want to die; I just didn't want to get fat. There had to be another way out. There just had to be.

Well, forty minutes later, we arrived at Somerset Medical Center. I didn't like the looks of it. Within minutes, I had already made up my mind that I wasn't going to stay there, no matter what.

My parents walked me into a small brick building located right next door to the main hospital. As soon as we entered, they walked me down a long corridor to a psychiatrist's office and left me inside while they stayed in the waiting room. I sat in silence, staring out the window, crossing and uncrossing my bony legs, wondering what was about to happen.

"They can't leave me here," I thought to myself. "I'm not sick enough. I weigh too much to be here. I'm sure there are girls that are much skinnier; who are much sicker than I. Therapy is not going to help anyway. I have to help myself. This sucks. They're probably going weigh me too. Ugh! I don't want to know how much I weigh! I cannot wait to go home and sleep."

Click…click. The door to the office opened and a middle-aged man carrying a clipboard wondered into the room. "Hello, there. I'm Dr. Danford," he introduced himself in an upbeat manner. "So, Jennifer, what brings you here?" he casually questioned.

"Uh, my parents?" I slyly answered. I wasn't going to make this easy.

"Well, why do you think they brought you here?" he asked.

"Um, I don't know. I guess they think I have some problem with eating," I replied.

"Well, let me ask you a few questions so I can understand why they might think that," he continued. He then proceeded to talk to me for about an hour, asking me about my habits, thoughts, feelings, and so on. I couldn't wait to leave. He explained what the eating disorders program had to offer and what it would entail.

After he weighed me, at a whopping eighty-nine pounds, he stated that it would be in my best interest if I stayed at the hospital, as an inpatient, for at least a few weeks. But he reminded me that he couldn't make me stay. He also stated that it wouldn't make sense for me to stay if I didn't have any interest in getting better. But if there was just one tiny part of me that wanted to get better, then I should give it a try.

I proceeded to contemplate the decision. There was a small part of me, deep down inside, that wanted to get better. I just didn't want to gain the weight. I finally told him my decision. "I'll stay, because part of me wants to get better," I declared. "But I'm not going to eat anything. That's the deal."

Of course, this didn't make sense. I obviously couldn't get better if I didn't eat anything. That's like an alcoholic going into an AA program with a bottle of vodka. Deep down, I knew I would have to eat.

"Jennifer, I can't guarantee that you will be able to skip meals. But we'll try to work out a reasonable plan for both of us," he said.

Well, for some reason I decided to agree to this. Part of me was relieved, and part of me was ashamed. I was giving in. I was giving up my control and my identity. But I was exhausted and was surprisingly ready for change. I wanted to go to college, and I knew I couldn't go if things stayed the way they were.

So I reluctantly walked out of the office with the doctor and he told my parents my decision. They seemed relieved. But I felt angry, hurt, confused, and most of all, betrayed.

How could my parents do this to me? How could they trick me into coming to this institution, miles and miles from our house? How could they just leave me there? Didn't they care about me? Didn't they want me to be happy? Leaving me at this strange place with all of these strange people wasn't going to make me happy. My own flesh and blood had drastically let me down.

We left the brick building and made our way over to the main hospital. After approximately thirty minutes of filing paperwork and signing consent forms, we were finally on our way up to the eating disorder wing.

"Well, here we are," Dr. Danford stated nonchalantly. "These are what the rooms look like. There are twelve inpatients here now, so you'll have to take one of these other rooms temporarily until a space is opened."

He continued the tour of the wing by unveiling the dining area and common room where the one TV was located. The common room was also where they held group sessions, nutrition class, and tutoring, if the patients were in school. And lastly, located right outside the common room was the kitchen.

Dr. Danford proceeded to inform me that we could save some of our food throughout the day in the kitchen if we couldn't eat it all and have it for snack. Immediately, I asked myself, "Why on earth would anyone voluntarily save food for later? That is just plain crazy."

At the end of the hallway, past the kitchen and common room, were the remaining patient rooms that were yet to be renovated. These rooms were still set up as regular hospital rooms, complete with white walls, white tile floors, and white sheets. My bed even had wheels.

I threw my suitcase up on my bed and took out my book of crossword puzzles. All I wanted was to be left alone. By now it was four thirty, and we would be having dinner in about an hour. My parents meandered throughout my room, stalling their goodbyes. I could tell they didn't want to leave me there.

"I'll be fine," I muttered, gazing into my mother's eyes, trying to play into her guilty conscious.

With tears running down her rosy cheeks, she embraced my bony body and whispered, "I love you. You know this is for your own good. We want to see you healthy again."

Deep down, I knew she was right. My dad gave me a quick hug and they were then finally on their way. I couldn't even look at them. Tears were streaming down my face as I dove into my pillow. I couldn't believe that it had come to this.

At that moment, it finally hit me. At last, reality had set in. I realized that there must have been something wrong with me. Normal people do not have to be admitted to a medical center. I had a serious problem. Starving myself was no longer a game. It was a sickness, and I had been brought here to get help. I just had to decide if I really wanted it or not.

I took a few deep breaths to stop the tears. I sat up and took a good look around. I noticed that there was a video camera in the upper right-hand corner of my room, directly behind the door. I assumed the purpose of these cameras was to ensure we did not try to exercise or purge. I felt so violated. I no longer had any privacy. I no longer had any control. I think that was the thing I feared the most. Losing the control.

A few minutes later, just after I started my first crossword puzzle, a group of girls walked into my room to say hello. After they briefly introduced themselves, they asked me a bunch of questions including how I was doing, how old I was, where I was from, and why I was there.

At first, I was reluctant to answer anything. I wasn't exactly in the mood to socialize. But I casually answered each of their questions with quick, one-word answers.

"Okay...seventeen...Morris County, New Jersey... anorexia," I replied.

I couldn't believe I actually said that word. Anorexia. I was always so reluctant to label myself with that term. To me, someone with anorexia weighed fifty pounds and never ate anything.

I, on the other hand, didn't have enough control to get that thin. I enjoyed food so much that I always gave in to my desires every few weeks or so with a binge. Not only that, but I weighed too much to be anorexic. Eighty-nine pounds was definitely not skinny enough.

There was no way that I was as sick as these other girls. They looked much thinner that I did. They had to be sicker than me. My guess is that they were probably laughing inside, thinking that I was way too fat to be there. That's definitely what they were thinking.

"How old are you?" I quietly asked the group. All four of them were between the ages of fourteen and sixteen. I was surprised. They all looked much younger.

"There's a lot of variety in here. One woman is forty-five. And the first time I was in here was when I was eleven. This is my fourth time here," a girl named Rita said.

Wow, I couldn't believe that she had started so young. And that she had been here before.

"Do most people come back after their first time in?" I asked.

"Yeah, not many people make it out of here in just one shot," she replied. "Most people have to come back in a few times before they really get better."

"Great," I thought to myself. "Is this what I have to look forward to for the next few years?" I didn't want to be in and out of a hospital for the rest of my life. I had to try to nip it in the bud this first time around. I just wanted to get on with the rest of my life.

We finally finished our small talk, and the girls left me to finish getting settled before dinner. It seemed like I would be in the hospital forever. Every minute seemed like an hour. The thought of dinner consumed my mind. Minute by minute I tried to come up with a plan that would eliminate me from having to go to the dinner table. Nothing. My mind drew a blank. There was no escaping. I would have to go to dinner and eat. Anxiety. Fear. Frustration. I couldn't do it. I just couldn't do it.

"Jen, dinner's here," one girl politely came in to remind me.

"Great. Wonderful. Just peachy," I thought. "What can I do?

As I slowly approached the dining area, I could see each inpatient gladly taking their trays off the rack and bringing them to the table. Why were they all so calm and collected? And why on earth did they look happy? This wasn't a happy occasion. They were going to have to eat food, and, on top of that, have to keep it down. I didn't understand. I would never be this way. I would never actually enjoy eating.

"C'mon dear, your tray is right here," one of the nurses stated.

I took one look at her and started to cry. The tears were uncontrollable. I bent over and practically sat on the floor.

"I can't do it. I'm sorry," I mumbled in between breaths. "I'm so sorry."

"It's ok, dear," the nurse said. "Just do what you can do. Take it step by step. I'll get you some tea."

I stayed outside in the hall with the nurse for ten minutes or so, sipping my tea. I was embarrassed to show my face after my meltdown. I hadn't even met some of the inpatients yet, and now they all knew me as the crybaby. But the nurse tried to convince me that everyone understood how I was feeling and held no judgment whatsoever. Then Rita came outside to check on me and asked me to come back in with her. I finally caved in and proceeded back into the dining area with Rita, with only my cup of tea in hand.

It was a bit crowded in the dining area because the room was made to fit about eight to ten inpatients; instead, we had thirteen. I squeezed myself in and glanced around at the happy faces. Again I thought to myself, "How could these people be enjoying this torturous event?" I just couldn't imagine feeling happy about food. It didn't seem possible.

I sat in silence and casually sipped my tea, wondering how many calories I would be consuming with the drop of milk I had added to it. Everyone else chatted and chuckled while devouring their entire meals that were placed in front of them. I simply observed. I couldn't fathom how I was going to be able to do this, three times a day, for at least the next few weeks. Especially if I was going to have to consume more than tea.

Once dinner was over, I quickly retreated back to my hospital room and continued to work on my crossword puzzles while waiting for snack time. I wasn't in much of a socializing mood. Two hours later, everyone grabbed their daily leftovers and retreated back to the dining area for their last meal of the day. Again, I just sat there while they all chatted and ate.

I still couldn't understand how they were enjoying this. Especially because having a snack was completely optional. Maybe at some point I would relate to them, but as of now, I never thought I would be able to eat in a relaxed fashion like they did.

As soon as they were finished with their food, we all went back to Rita's room. They continued to ask me some questions and I finally began to open up. I, too, asked questions, especially about eating here at the hospital.

"How come you guys enjoy eating so much? Doesn't it bother you?" I asked.

"Of course it bothers us, just not as much anymore," they replied. "We know that if we eat, we can go out on pass this weekend."

This meant that if they gained enough weight they could leave the hospital for a few hours to visit family and friends. But you could only gain this privilege after being there for at least a week, so I had absolutely no chance of getting out on pass that first weekend. But I was hoping that I could get out the following weekend since it was my birthday on Saturday. And I knew I'd have to eat in order to do so.

Another privilege that I would have to wait for was leaving the unit. I couldn't leave the unit for forty-eight hours. The others could leave the unit, during free time, for no more than twenty-five minutes. During this twenty-five minute period, most of the inpatients would go for walks or go to the gift shop. I couldn't wait for this privilege. I was just itching to get back outside.

Unfortunately, the girls also informed me of some unit penalties. During the times that I wasn't gaining weight, I would be forced to "bed rest" for the day, or in some cases, a few days at a time. While on bed rest, I could only go to meals and group therapy sessions. Other than that, I would have to stay in my bed at all times. And in drastic cases, I'd have to be fed through a feeding tube.

I was suddenly realizing that I was going to have to eat and gain some weight in order to have some sense of normalcy during my stay there. I didn't want to be confined to my bed, or even worse, be fed through a plastic tube against my will. But even if I wanted to eat, I wouldn't be able to go through with it. The thought of food crossing my lips disgusted me. I couldn't bear the thought of chewing, never mind swallowing. But deep down I knew I was going to have to get over this fear quickly if I wanted to get out of this place any time soon.

I finally went to bed around midnight and was soon awakened by one of the nurses. At six a.m. the knock came on my door. I was not prepared for how early we had to wake up, but the nurses needed time to do their rounds before breakfast. All thirteen patients had to be weighed and have their blood pressure taken. I was not happy, but had no choice.

I reluctantly draped the blue and white polka-dotted hospital gown over my emaciated body. As I tied the robe shut, I could feel my hip bone sticking out. Deep down, I knew it wasn't normal. To confirm this realization, I reached my left hand around to my right side and felt my ribcage. I could easily count every rib bone as I slide my hand down my side. That definitely wasn't normal.

These thoughts were strange because for the first time I was able to admit to myself that I wasn't fat. Maybe my mind was playing tricks on me. I knew that I shouldn't be able to see that many bones protruding through my skin. I was practically a walking skeleton. But even though I could feel my bones, I still felt fat.

I took a quick glance in the mirror, and I still saw a fat girl. I couldn't see that I was skinny. Only by physically touching my skin and feeling the protruding bones did I realize that my body wasn't normal. I just didn't get it.

Why did I still look and feel so disgustingly fat when I only weighed eighty-nine pounds? Maybe if I lost a few more pounds I would finally look skinny. Just a few more pounds. That's what I had been saying all along. And now I was stuck here in the hospital where I was going to have to gain weight. There was nothing I could do about it now, so I finished closing my gown and walked down to meet the nurse at the scale.

"Alright, Jennifer, step up here," Patty, one of the nurses on staff, said.

The scale wasn't a typical gray doctor's office scale. There was a large square stainless steel base, which I had to step onto, and it was connected to a digital box that stood about eye-level, where my weight would be displayed. Luckily, there was a large pink piece of paper taped over the numbers so I could not see my weight.

I slowly stepped up onto the scale and Patty cautiously lifted up the pink slip of paper to record my weight. Of course, I was dying to know if I had lost any weight since the previous day. Then again, if I had gained weight, I didn't want to know. Regardless, it didn't matter because she wasn't allowed to tell me. I got down and quickly returned to my warm cozy bed, where I was able to catch a few more minutes of sleep before I had to start my day.

Ten minutes went by and I forced myself to get out of bed again. I gathered my towel, clothes, and toiletries and headed for the shower. This would be yet another interesting venture.

The showers were located sporadically throughout the unit and looked just like linen closets. I had to have one of the nurses unlock the shower door. I also had to ask for my razor, which was kept behind the desk for safety precautions just in case I had the urge after eating to cut myself like I had done so many times before. I was only allowed to have it during my shower.

After showering, I got dressed and joined the others in the common room. Breakfast came up on the trays at seven a.m. Once again, everyone seemed to enjoy finding their tray and discovering what they had ordered for that particular morning like it was buried treasure.

I, on the other hand, didn't even choose what I was going to eat. The nutritionist had chosen my meals for me. Yogurt, cereal, a banana, milk, and juice were all on my tray. "What are they, crazy?" I thought to myself. "They are all absolutely insane. I could never possibly consume that much in one sitting. There was easily a month's worth of calories on that tray."

Overwhelmed with anxiety, I tried to keep calm as I ventured back into the common room with my tray of a thousand calories. The thirteen of us squeezed in around the long table, and I patiently sipped my juice, waiting for breakfast to be over. Even though everyone else was eating and chatting, I felt like all eyes were on me.

It seemed as if everyone was watching me sip the juice. And they were thinking, "I can't believe she's actually drinking that juice. It has calories, just like food. What a disappointment. She has absolutely no willpower. She should know by now that you should never drink calories. It's a waste of time. If you're going to consume calories it might as well be actual food, not just a wimpy glass of juice. Gosh, she is so pathetic. No willpower whatsoever."

Okay, so maybe they weren't thinking this. But I was. I was so ashamed that I was giving in. I couldn't believe that I was taking in actual calories. But at least it was something, and the nurses could see I was trying. That's all that mattered. I didn't want to be force fed by a feeding tube, so I had to try my hardest.

Once breakfast was over, I met with Britney, one of the nutritionists, to go over my meals. I was sitting on my bed trying to decide what to do when Britney entered with a fistful of green paper menus in one hand and a food pyramid in the other.

She quickly announced, "Jennifer, Dr. Danford has informed me that you will begin on the 1200-calorie diet. Each day, you will need to consume six servings of bread/grains, three servings of dairy, three fruits/vegetables, three proteins, and one fat. Here is a chart of serving equivalents. If you need any extra help, Rita knows most of the basics, but I'll try to help you get started. Let's start with today's lunch...how 'bout tuna fish? Do you like tuna fish? Here, see, you can circle tuna fish here and write '½ cup' beside it so they know how much to give you. And if you like tu—"

"No!" I exclaimed, rudely interrupting her. "I can't imagine eating tuna fish! You don't understand. I can't eat that stuff. I can't imagine eating anything right now. Why don't you just fill it out for me? It would be so much quicker. It doesn't matter what you write down. I'm probably not going to eat it anyway."

"Jennifer, you're going to have to fill these menus out every week. You should start getting used to it," Britney replied. "It's better that you choose stuff that you like because you're eventually going to have to eat it anyway."

"I guess you're right," I said, after a large sigh. "I just have no idea what it feels like to actually crave food. And I'm never hungry. I guess I'll just have to choose things that I used to enjoy eating when I was younger."

I took the menus for the rest of the week and filled them out according to my meal plan. It was pretty frustrating. I couldn't imagine eating any of the food that I was circling. But I knew I would eventually be forced to.

Once ten a.m. rolled around, we were all instructed to head into the common room for nutrition class. All of the outpatients had arrived by this point. Most of them had been inpatients at one time and were now on the road to recovery out in the real world. Outpatients came to the hospital multiple times throughout the week, some more than others depending on the need.

The inpatients and outpatients combined for nutrition class and group therapy on Mondays, Wednesdays, and Fridays. This worked well because the inpatients were able to hear about the outpatients' experiences back in the real world and how they were dealing with recovery.

Nutrition class was plain and simple. It covered stuff that you learned all throughout grammar school. We went over the food pyramid and the different serving sizes. The funny thing was that we all knew about nutrition. We probably knew more than most people did about calorie counting and had read more nutrition labels than everyone on the planet.

We knew what our bodies needed. We knew what we were doing wasn't healthy. We just didn't care. We thought we were invincible. We felt that our bodies were different than everybody else's. We felt that we didn't need food to live. I know this sounds strange, but this was my thought process. Half of me knew that I needed to eat; the other half believed that food was bad. Just where was my rationale?

I had no rationale. I sat there, while everyone else disputed over the calorie content of fish, and doodled on the handout about protein that was given to us. "Eating meat is a waste of time," I thought to myself. "If I'm going to eat something, it's going to be macaroni and cheese or mashed potatoes, something of that nature. Or, better yet, mint chocolate chip ice cream. Or perhaps a huge piece of chocolate cake. Yum."

I couldn't decide what sounded better. I had deprived myself of food for so long I wouldn't know what to do with myself if I was presented with all of these foods at once. Whenever I did eat, I would only allow myself one thing at a time. Having to choose among a host of different foods that I liked would be tough.

"That's why it was just so much easier eating a little of everything and then throwing it up," I thought to myself. "I got to enjoy all of the tasty dishes without having to deal with the calories. So my throat got a little raw and my hands were all scraped up from sticking my fingers down my throat. So what? It was all worth it, right? I mean, I was skinnier than most people. Well, I mean, don't get me wrong. I still had pounds to lose before I could be considered skinny, but still. I had it all under control."

Well, of course, until now. Now, I was forced to sit here in this boring nutrition class, learning stuff I already knew but just didn't want to adhere to, and I wasn't having any fun. I didn't know how much more of this I was going to be able to take.

An hour had gone by and it was finally time for group therapy. But first, we were instructed to take our meds. Medications were a new concept for me. It was hard for me to believe that a pill could make me happy, but at this point I was willing to try anything.

During my initial discussions with Dr. Danford, he had recommended that I go on a number of medications. I started with an antidepressant called Paxil, along with Ambien, which was a drug that would help me sleep at night. Additionally, he put me on Colace, which would help my digestion system, since I had been abusing laxatives for so long.

Once everyone's meds were handed out, we filed back into the common room for "group," as they referred to it. There must have been about twenty women all together. We started the meeting off by going around the room and stating our name and a number from one to ten which reflected how we were feeling that day. Ten meant great while one meant shitty.

Most of the inpatients categorized themselves as twos and threes, while most of the outpatients chose sevens and eights. It varied, of course, but for the most part, the outpatients were further along in their recovery and thus had a more optimistic approach to their current situation.

When it came to be my turn, I barely whispered, "I'm Jennifer and I would say I'm about a two today."

The basis for group therapy was to give everyone an open forum to discuss a current issue, whether it was in regards to relationships, school, work, or family. It didn't matter. The only requirement was that it should not focus on food. And talking was strictly voluntary. All I knew was that I was not going to open my mouth and share my problems with a bunch of strangers. I was just going to sit there and keep my mouth shut.

Ninety minutes slowly ticked by. I desperately tried to listen intently to the other girls while they spoke about their problems in order to take my mind off of the next meal. I must admit that listening to a few other girls who were dealing with food issues helped a little. Hearing their stories led me to believe that perhaps I really was sick and that I did need help.

Lunch finally came, and again I only drank a small cup of apple juice. I looked at all the food on my tray and glanced up at all the people who surrounded me. This time, my company not only included the twelve other inpatients, but the fifteen outpatients as well. I just couldn't handle all of those eyes staring at me while I ate, so I opted for the juice.

The juice, just by itself, gave me anxiety. It had calories, and somehow I thought I would gain weight from it. I was convinced of this. Perhaps I could just keep drinking juice and gain some weight that way. Then I wouldn't have to deal with food. Sounded like a compromise to me.

Unfortunately, the nurses and nutritionists disagreed. Patty pulled me aside after lunch and warned me, "Jennifer, you're going to have to eat solid food soon. Otherwise, we're going to have to put you on a feeding tube. You're not getting the calories that you need to survive."

"Okay, okay. I'll try at dinner. I promise," I reluctantly replied.

What the hell was I going to eat? I couldn't possibly eat steak and mashed potatoes! I only had the next four hours to figure it out. I couldn't imagine putting anything in my mouth. This was going to be tough.

I needed a distraction. I decided to make a phone call to one of my friends. As I was on the phone, I couldn't help but notice a girl named Kiera stepping onto the treadmill that was located on the unit, right next to the phones. And right next to the treadmill was a Stairmaster and a stationary bike. I couldn't believe they actually had exercise equipment on the premises!

This didn't make sense. Usually those with eating disorders have abnormally vigorous exercise schedules as well, which aren't healthy. But, apparently, I later found out that depending on your weight, you were allowed exercise privileges during your stay. Some of the bulimics were normal weight so they were free to exercise for a limited amount of time each day. In addition, there were a few overeaters on the unit who were also allowed exercise priveleges and who honestly needed to. Unfortunately, as an underweight anorexic, I didn't weigh enough to get those privileges.

But watching Kiera, who was diagnosed as a bulimic, made me realize that she was very obsessed with exercise. Even though her weight was okay, she had major issues with her appearance that were not healthy. I hoped the nurses and doctors were able to see this. From my standpoint, her obsession with exercise was just as bad as the binging and purging and should be dealt with accordingly.

Dinnertime quickly came. Part of me was a bit nervous, but another part of me was excited. I hadn't eaten in so long, so I couldn't wait to actually taste something. I had decided the easiest thing for me to eat would be crackers and peanut butter. I remembered how much I used to love peanut butter when I was little. And even though roast beef and mashed potatoes came up on my tray, the nutritionist made an exception by giving me my special request, which they always had in the kitchen.

Putting the first cracker in my mouth was torture. It felt very strange. I wasn't hungry, and I wasn't really in the mood for it. But I slowly chewed and swallowed four whole saltines, coated with peanut butter. I tried not to look up from my tray to prevent making eye contact, and once dinner was finished, I quickly ran back into my room and began to cry.

I felt like such a failure. "What was I thinking?" I thought to myself.

I was going to gain so much weight. I just knew it. My stomach felt so huge! The calories were just seeping into my veins. I couldn't handle it. I felt so gross. And no one could understand. It seemed like everyone else was eating and not worrying about it. For me, it was the only thing I could think about. My mind was so focused on the food and the calories and the fat and my body. Not to mention my weight. I was certain that the numbers were about to go up because of what I ate. And the very next day I had the chance to find out.

I woke up the next morning at six a.m. and made the daily routine walk down the hallway to get weighed. Later that morning, in nutrition class, Britney came in and handed me a little piece of paper folded in half.

"What's this?" I softly whispered to a girl sitting next to me.

"That's your weight," she replied. "They give it to you three times a week. You can choose to look at it or not. It's up to you."

I was almost positive that I had gained weight. Most of me believed that eating those crackers had made me gain weight, but there was a small rational part of me that knew I probably couldn't have gained weight from digesting less than one hundred calories. Regardless, I couldn't stand the uncertainty. I had to know.

So, slowly but surely, making sure no one was looking, I opened the little slip of paper and saw "89" scribbled on a small dotted line at the bottom of the slip. I didn't lose weight.

"God dammit!" I immediately thought to myself. "That damn juice. I knew it had too many calories."

Lunch was approaching soon, and all I could think about was what I was going to eat. Did I want to have crackers and peanut butter again? Or should I try something different? But if I tried something else, would that make me gain weight? Decisions, decisions.

Our trays came up and bread, yogurt, fruit, cereal, and milk covered mine. Again, I was completely overwhelmed and anxious. Deep down, I knew I had to eat something; otherwise, I'd be threatened with a feeding tube. I watched the other girls, and most of them began their meals by having a bowl of cereal. It looked easy, so I figured I'd take my chances and do the same thing.

I opened a box of plain Cheerios, poured them into a small plastic bowl, and added a splash of skim milk. Of course, I tried to use as little milk as possible to keep the calories down. It was hard to envision eating this whole bowl of cereal without throwing it up. I wasn't used to eating a normal helping of food; usually I either had a few bites of something or binged on a huge portion of junk food. Rarely did I eat anything inbetween.

But because I had tasted the crackers, I could sense what the taste of cereal would be like. With my stomach tied in knots, I took the first spoonful, trying not to think about the amount of calories I was consuming. I chewed slowly, constantly reminding myself that eating was normal and that it was a good thing. It was truly hard to imagine a life of eating without obsessing about it, but if these girls could do it, I had hope I could too.

As a distraction, I tried to concentrate on the conversations that were going on around me. Kiera kept bugging the nursing assistant to let her exercise. Rita kept complaining about her family meetings, which I would have to start having soon as well. And Silvia, a forty-year-old woman with fake teeth and hardly any hair left on her head, kept complaining about her husband, who was trying to divorce her. "Maybe my problems aren't so bad after all," I thought to myself.

As I sat there and listened intently to these girls, I began to realize that many of them had been going through this for quite some time, especially Silvia. She had been in five different hospitals throughout her life and had been suffering from anorexia and bulimia for over twenty-five years.

"How could anyone suffer that long?" I pondered. "I don't understand how anyone could get wrapped up in the disease for that amount of time."

Seven years had been long enough for me. I couldn't stand being sick any more, and now that I'd seen the effects of what this illness could do long-term, I definitely wanted to get better.

Silvia had lost most of her hair; it was long and curly but very thin. And all of her teeth had fallen out due to the effects of the bulimia. She now had to wear dentures at the age of forty. In addition, her husband was divorcing her and was also trying to declare full custody of their two twin five-year-old boys. He claimed that she wouldn't be able to take care of them since she could barely take care of herself.

"Do I want to end up like this?" I sat there, asking myself. "Of course not."

I wanted to live a long, happy life, with a husband and children, not in-and-out of hospitals dealing with my insurance company. Silvia barely weighed fifty-five pounds. I couldn't even fathom how she was walking around the unit. And she never once fainted. I could barely walk down to my room and back without getting tired. A small part of me was partially jealous of her weight and her control, but a larger part of me knew that being like her was not something to envy.

With all of the distractions that the conversation created, I successfully finished my bowl of cereal without a drop to spare. It wasn't easy, but I was happy with my accomplishment. I didn't feel overly full, so that helped. It was a small step, but a step in the right direction for sure.

Over the next few days, I went through the daily routine of getting weighed, going to nutrition class and group therapy sessions, and meeting with my psychiatrist, psychologist, and social worker, as well as doing schoolwork. In my spare time I began bonding quickly with the other patients, young and old. I consistently ate two things at each meal. Yogurt with fruit, crackers with peanut butter, or cereal in yogurt: these were the only three things I would allow myself to have. They were simple and low in calories.

By Friday, I had gained one pound. I couldn't believe it. I felt like I had gained ten pounds, not just one. I was bloated and constipated, which led to much discomfort. I wasn't used to digesting food, never mind excreting it without laxatives. Between therapy and eating, I was mentally exhausted and physically in pain.

Feeling anything was not something I was used to. I was used to being empty. I was used to being numb, but now I was feeling physical pain. And on top of that, unfortunately I was feeling emotional pain as well.

I hated having to feel again. I was angry with my parents. I missed my friends, which made me sad. I was nervous about finishing school and gaining weight. It was incredibly confusing and frustrating, trying to figure out what I was actually feeling and why. Needless to say, I was overwhelmed. I missed the feeling of emptiness that obscurity had given me.

As I lay on my bed writing in my journal, I came to a strikingly obvious revelation. Every time I became overwhelmed with emotion, I would focus on my body. It seemed that every emotion related to how I felt about my weight. I just couldn't figure out why, but I was determined to piece it together.

Every time I started thinking about my parents and how angry I was at them, I felt fat. Each time I reflected on how much work I had to catch up on for school, I would suddenly obsess over a body part, whether it be my big thighs or fat ass. I began to realize that focusing on my body and my weight helped take the focus off the other things that were going on in my life, like schoolwork and family problems. I guess this made sense, but now I had to figure out how I could solve this problem. That was the hard part.

On Monday, a week into my hospital stay, my entire family came down to the hospital for our first therapy session together. My parents and sister greeted me at the entrance to the unit. Although I was still angry with how my parents handled the situation, I was still excited to see familiar faces and to have my family there.

Next to the entrance was my new room. One of the inpatients was going home and I was able to move in to her spot. I was excited since I was now able to move out of my hospital-like room, where I was all alone, and into this carpeted and colorful room, where I would have an actual roommate.

In my mind, I began planning how I would decorate my new room as I walked with my family into a small office where my social worker, Dina, was waiting. As we were seated, I crossed my right leg over my left. In doing so, I was able to tuck my right foot under my left leg since my legs were so thin.

My father wittingly commented, "I wish I could do that."

At that moment, part of me felt amazingly special. Not many others could do this, but I could. As silly as that sounds, it did make me feel special, which in my mind was a positive thing. However, I didn't realize, or perhaps did but didn't want to admit, that being able to cross my legs like that meant that I was sickly thin. I was unhealthy and able to bend my body in ways that it wasn't meant to be bent. I know that making this comment was my dad's way saying I was too thin, but unfortunately I didn't interpret it that way. The comment certainly stuck with me.

The entire session lasted for about an hour. Dina started off asking a few questions, which fueled the fire, especially with my mom. The focus quickly shifted off of me and my eating disorder and onto the issues my mom had with my dad. Everyone was uncomfortable and remained silent for the most part while my mother continued with her rant.

We had never discussed my parent's issues before. They never fought, but at the same time, they never laughed together either. They hung out together when I was little, but as my sister and I grew up they seemed to grow apart.

I had known that my mother had been unhappy in their marriage for some time, and perhaps that is what had bothered me so. Perhaps if my mother had divorced my father when I was young, seeing her happy may have been better for me. It's hard to judge, because at the same time I enjoyed the family trips and holidays. Those occasions would have been much different if they were divorced, so again, it's tough to imagine how life could have been. We could only move forward.

After we finished the family session, my family left and I made my way back into my room to work on my new needlepoint project. It was hard to digest everything that had been said that evening. I wasn't quite sure what to make of it since my father and sister didn't really speak. I ignored my thoughts and focused on the craft at hand. Crafts helped to relax me.

As I finished up one of the flowers on the needlepoint, I used the tiny sewing scissors to cut the thread. Holding those sharp little shears reminded me of the times I cut myself in the shower. I remembered how good it felt to feel the physical pain and how it distracted me from the discomfort of eating.

At that moment, for whatever reason, I began scraping the palm of my hand with the tiny blades. It felt so good to feel pain. I scraped and scraped and scraped until I started to bleed. It stung but felt enjoyable at the same time. It had taken my mind off of the family therapy session that had just occurred.

Surprisingly, one of the other girls noticed my hand the next morning and asked me what had happened. I told her, thinking that she would understand and keep it as our little secret. But I was wrong.

She quickly brought it to the attention of one of the nurses. They immediately took away my scissors and reported the incident to my doctors. The psychologist that was working with me brought it up later that morning in hopes of linking it back to a specific emotion I had been feeling at the time. It was hard to figure out the specific reason, but it was clearly the first time I realized that I was acting out due to my emotions.

I felt like such a psycho. "Who did this kind of stuff?" I asked myself. I didn't understand. I had never heard of anyone else cutting themselves, so where the hell did I get this idea?

The only rational reason that I could find was that it was a way for me to feel. Perhaps I didn't express my feelings at the family therapy session, so afterwards I cut myself in order to feel. At this point, it had become clear to me that this was no longer a punishment for eating. It was an emotional release. I was sad, angry, frustrated and most of all, disappointed in my family and even more so in myself. But these feelings were ugly feelings so therefore, dealing with the physical pain was easier than the emotional.

By Wednesday, I started to feel more at ease with the hospital and the other patients. I had finally settled in. We had a daily routine, which helped set my expectations, and everyone was very friendly, including the doctors, nurses, and all the other patients.

I had moved from my old hospital room into a colorful carpeted room with Jackie, a thirty-year-old woman who was still living at home with her mother prior to coming into the hospital. Although we had a thirteen-year age gap between us, it was extremely easy to relate to her issues and feelings.

We both watched the same soap operas, enjoyed listening to '80s pop music, and also surprisingly enjoyed talking about food, especially about how much we missed eating the "bad" stuff like ice cream, cookies, and candy. We hated having to eat "healthy" foods without being able to eat the junk. We swore that once we both recovered from our eating disorders we would go out for ice cream sundaes. I couldn't even imagine what that would be like, but I really hoped that I could get there.

Kiera, the exercise addict, told us that she did feel comfortable eating the bad stuff, but we weren't so sure. Even though she was at a decent weight, her body image was completely skewed. She had the doctors, even most of the other patients, completely fooled. However, on Wednesday, her secrets were revealed.

The night before, Kiera's roommate requested that she be moved out of their room due to her aggressive and high-strung personality. Kiera was placed in my old room, alone. However, Wednesday morning, another patient checked into the hospital and was stuck rooming with Kiera until another opportunity opened up.

The new girl's name was Linda, and she closely observed Kiera's habits during her first day there and reported them to the other girls. Apparently, Kiera had been vomiting after every meal in her room into a water bottle hidden in her locker.

Linda figured it out due to the wretched smell the bottles were creating in their room.

A bunch of us, including Patty, the nurse, decided to confront Kiera as a group about this secret. We anxiously proceeded to enter her room and open her locker while she watched in disbelief.

"What the hell do you think you're doing?" she exclaimed.

As we were trying to comfort her and ask some questions, I began to think about lunch, since it was almost that time. I suddenly became lightheaded and was breathing much quicker than usual. At first I didn't want to say anything, since I was used to feeling weak and lethargic. That was how I felt every day before I started eating again.

But after about a minute I began to feel tingly and faint, and worst of all, the air felt too thick to breathe. Trying not to cause a commotion, I casually mentioned that I felt a bit weak, but I must have looked extremely pale because the nurse came running to my side almost as if she was going to catch me from falling. I bent over as the room began to spin and practically disappear in darkness.

The nurse kept saying, "Deep breaths. Just keep taking deep breaths."

"Why can't I breathe?" I thought to myself. "Why do I feel so nervous all of a sudden? Am I having an asthma attack? I never had asthma before in my life. How is this possible?"

One of the other nurses overheard us and grabbed a brown paper bag. She brought it over to me and told me to breathe as slowly and deeply as I could into it. As soon as I began to breathe at a normal pace, the nurse escorted me into my room, where I laid down on my bed and began to cry.

I couldn't understand what had happened. Apparently, I had experienced a panic attack, which I had never even heard of before. Patty suggested that the anxiety towards eating lunch may have triggered the attack. I certainly hoped this was a one-time occurrence and was not going to happen again, but deep down I knew the anxiety wasn't going anywhere.

And I see your true colors shining through
I see your true colors
And that's why I love you
So don't be afraid
To let them show
Your true colors
Your true colors are beautiful like a rainbow.

–Cyndi Lauper, "True Colors"

6 | i'm free

The following Saturday arrived, and because I hadn't gained enough weight, I did not receive a pass to leave the hospital. Not only did I not receive a pass, but I was also put on bed rest, which meant I could only leave my bed for meals and to go to the bathroom. So this was how I would spend my eighteenth birthday.

Luckily, everyone tried to make me forget I was even in the hospital. Most of the girls got ready early and decorated the Eating Disorder Unit (a.k.a. the EDU) with balloons and banners that said "Happy Birthday, Jennifer," and at breakfast, some of them presented me with gifts and cards. Getting this much attention from people I barely even knew was extremely overwhelming, but in a very good way.

My family also joined me later that day to help me celebrate. Visiting hours on Saturday did not begin until after lunch, so before they arrived, I had some time to relax and journal in my room. My lucky roommate Jackie received a six-hour pass, so she left shortly after breakfast. I finally had some time alone to reflect.

As I sat on my bed and hung up my birthday cards next to the surplus of other get-well cards I had received, I began to realize how many people loved me and cared about me. My aunts, uncles, cousins, friends, and teachers had all sent cards and letters wishing me their best. Additionally, classmates and family members who I barely knew or communicated with sent me cards full of well wishes. Maybe they were trying to tell me something. Maybe they saw me as something more than just a skinny person. Maybe they honestly liked having me as a part of their life and loved me for who I was, not just the scrawny little girl they saw on the surface.

I honestly was starting to believe that I was more than just a skinny person. I just couldn't remember who I was anymore, since I had wrapped my whole self-worth and reason for living around my eating disorder for the past seven years. Now I needed to figure that out.

One of the best recovery techniques that a therapist had shared earlier that week during our group session was a visualization exercise. In this exercise, we were to think back and recall a time when food was not an issue. This would potentially help us remember what it was like to not focus our entire existence around food, and it would also help us recall what activities we used to enjoy before the eating disorder developed.

Obviously, this was a challenging exercise for most of us, since it felt as though we had been obsessed with food over the course of our entire life. However, that morning, as I sat on my bed alone in my hospital room staring at the gifts and cards that hung on the wall, I realized that I did enjoy things other than counting calories. I had shared many different experiences with most of the people who had sent me those cards.

One of my favorites was getting Italian Ice every summer at the town pool. My mother would give me fifty cents each day to get some from the ice cream man. Oh, how I loved Italian

Ice. I would run to the ice cream truck as soon as I heard the bells ring. I never thought twice about how many calories were in a scoop. Why should I now?

As I ate the cherry-flavored treat, all I could think about was how good it tasted and how much I couldn't wait to get back in the pool. But now, in the same situation, not only would I be worried about how many calories I was consuming, I'd also be worried about how fat I looked in my bathing suit. Not once would I think about how much fun I was having at the pool.

This visualization exercise was ground-breaking because, for the first time, it helped me recall how happy I was not worrying about calories and fat content. I remembered how much more I had enjoyed life. I desired to be that way again. I needed to be that way again in order to be happy and healthy.

I took out my journal and began to write about my times as a child when food was something I looked forward to. When I was nine, I used to beg for a snack after school, which usually consisted of Doritos or Cheetos. And every night, without fail, I'd have my bowl of ice cream in front of the TV set, no questions asked. Each day at lunchtime, I'd look forward to reaching into my lunchbox to find out what great treat my mom had included.

"Was it a cupcake? Cookies? Yodels?" I'd wonder. Yodels were my favorite.

Food used to be such a great thing. Every Sunday after church, I would love going into Dunkin' Donuts to spend fifteen minutes selecting a donut. Strawberry frosted and vanilla cream-filled were my favorites. Not once did I consider how many calories were inside those items, nor did I think about how much exercise I would have to do in order to burn that donut off.

So why was I worrying now—especially when I was forty pounds underweight? Logically, I really couldn't make sense of it all. The only thing that made sense was that I was starving myself for attention. I was starving myself so people would notice me. I was starving myself so people would recognize that I was upset and that there was a problem. Now if I could just figure out the problem, we'd be all set.

My parents and relatives finally arrived shortly after lunch, which at this point was still yogurt and cereal for me. We spent the afternoon putting puzzles together and visiting in my room. After a few hours, they left and I spent the rest of the evening doing crosswords and needlepoint. This had to have been the most boring birthday ever. As I tucked myself into bed that night, I thought to myself, "This is the last birthday I am ever spending in a hospital."

A couple weeks passed and I had gained five pounds. I started branching out from my yogurt, cereal, and fruit diet to more substantial food such as eggs and vegetables. While this was certainly an achievement, I was having a hard time seeing the good.

I began to feel like I was losing control. I was losing control of what I was eating, how much weight I was gaining, and most importantly, I was losing my identity. I was losing a habit that had consumed my life. And, to me, this habit was what I did best and made me feel special, like it was the only thing that I was good at.

Due to this lack of control, I found myself quickly struggling to find things that I could control, such as cleaning. Cleaning my room and the entire EDU quickly became my new obsession. Not only was it something I could control, but it was also something that distracted me from dealing with the emotions that had been hidden for so long.

So I cleaned and organized everything. The hair brush and comb on my nightstand needed to be in certain positions. My cards that hung on the wall had to all line up with the same amount of space in between. My clothes and shoes always had to be put away. Everything had its place and I freaked out if it wasn't all there.

One evening, I spent three hours cleaning up the arts and crafts supplies, obsessing over every little crayon wrapper that was found in the pencil box. The nurses finally yelled at me to go to bed. They knew what I was doing, even though I didn't even realize it at the time. I honestly felt that I just liked being tidy. Not once did the fact that I was looking for another way to control something cross my mind.

After two weeks of being in the hospital, I realized that it was going to take longer than the doctor's original three-week estimate for me to venture back out into the real world. But as much as I wanted to be with my friends, I knew that this was my big chance to finally overcome this hideous disease. And it was the only chance I'd have to fight this thing before I went away to college.

Going off to college meant a great deal to me. I'd be on my own and able to start a whole new identity for myself—a new identity that didn't consist of me having an eating disorder. I had six months to kick this habit and I was determined. I did not want to miss out on any more of my life than I already had.

Jackie, who had been my roommate for the first couple weeks, was now being discharged from the unit. Although she would continue coming to outpatient therapy a few times a week, things would not be the same. Her optimism really seemed to keep me going. She constantly talked about how much she loved ice cream and cookies and all the other "bad" foods. I couldn't wait to meet up with her one day for an ice cream cone. It was a long way off, but I was optimistic that it would eventually happen.

Devon, one of the current outpatients, would be taking Jackie's place. Devon had been through a couple of inpatient hospitalizations already at other centers and had finally enrolled in the Somerset Outpatient Program just a few weeks before I had been admitted. She was a few years younger than me at the age of fifteen and was a gymnast on her high school team. Although I would miss Jackie, I was looking forward to having a roommate who was at the same place in the recovery process. We could go through the process together.

And luckily, the process was becoming easier and easier. Eating had become less of an issue even though I was gaining weight. Because I was gaining weight, my stomach was expanding, making it more comfortable to eat without feeling stuffed. I was also finding that I had more energy and was able to concentrate better. These positive side effects were forcing me to stay on track.

I was extremely conscious of what I was eating and only felt comfortable eating certain foods, but at least I was eating. Mealtimes, for me, started to focus more on the social aspect and less on the food aspect. As I continued to write in my journal each day, I began to write about food less and my feelings more. I even began to talk in the therapy group.

During my first couple weeks in the hospital, I usually labeled my mood as a one or a two when we went around the circle for introductions, but now I was up to about a three or four. Still not a ten. Very far from a ten, in fact. However, I was slowly but surely getting comfortable with the idea of getting better.

Dealing with my feelings was easier when I had others surrounding me who could relate. I finally realized this during my second week once I began getting to know the other inpatients. It was interesting to hear their stories and comforting to recognize that others were struggling with similar issues.

I especially looked forward to the time that we were allowed off the unit. Once we maintained a certain weight and had been admitted for over forty-eight hours, we were allowed off-unit privileges for a twenty-minute time period. At that time, we were permitted to go for walks throughout the hospital and outside. I found that when we were off the unit, everyone felt more open and free to discuss what was going on inside their heads. Our off-unit time brought everyone together.

The first time I was allowed out, Rita brought the vending machines to my attention. Everyone in the unit loved diet soda. It was the drink that most of us were used to consuming on a daily basis. However, the eating disorders unit did not allow diet sodas or any other food that contained Nutrasweet in the unit. They truly frowned upon any type of diet food and tried to make us focus on pure nutrition. Therefore, we would have to illegally drink it when we were not on the premises.

So during my first venture off the unit, Rita took a bunch of us over to the nearest vending machine, located in the ER lobby, and we sat and enjoyed cans of Diet Coke. And as we sat and drank the forbidden cola, I realized that I was, at that moment, experiencing freedom. Freedom from the eating disorder. Freedom from the hospital. I was free, out in the world, enjoying a soda with friends, and I was not, for the first time, thinking about food. And I loved it.

Diary Entry: 3/12/96

To My Stupid Disease:

I hate you! Because of you I have been living a nightmare for five years. Recently, you caused me to be admitted into Somerset Hospital to try and get rid of you. You've been my only real friend for so long. You were always there when I needed you. You always could get rid of my problems. And you gave me such a sense of control.

But it was all temporary. All you did was get rid of my emotions for a short period of time. Instead of the emotions coming out, they continued to get stuffed down inside. And now, all I deal with 24/7 are these feelings. It's totally been helping me to deal with you and not using and abusing you to deal with it.

I hate you so much. You have made me so scared of food. All I want to do is to eat and be normal. I've been at this hospital for three weeks today. I definitely have gotten stronger. I've been feeling better about eating while dealing with my feelings. It seems to be working, but I still have a ways to go.

Yesterday, I found out my parents are getting a divorce. I was so tempted to use you to deal with my feelings. I was so proud of myself for not doing it. I ate but felt really guilty. And although I did not starve or binge, I did hurt myself. I kept cutting myself over and over again with a razor blade. It felt so good to get out my anger, and to hurt myself.

Now I've just become one more step away from overcoming this stupid illness. I hate you! You've ruined my life. I wish you would just go away and never come back. You are so over-controlling—no one should ever suffer this much. Please go away. I need you to leave in order to survive. Please let others hear me when I need help.

Jen

Okay. So my parents were finally getting a divorce. Well, at least that's what my mother told me. Finally, she was doing it. She was finally ending the unhealthy relationship that she and my father had for years.

I could tell that they both loved each other, but they just didn't make each other happy. They didn't like the same things. They didn't laugh at the same jokes. They didn't have the same sense of humor. They were just different. And I had noticed it for years. Subconsciously, for the most part, but I still noticed it.

It unmistakably bothered me so much that it had added to the cause of my eating disorder. It upset me that I could not control their happiness and could not fix their relationship; therefore, I controlled how much food I put in my body.

Now that my mother had proclaimed her decision to divorce my father, I felt relieved but dejected. Although I knew that this was the best decision for both my mother and father, it was still hard to accept that my parents would no longer be husband and wife. They would now be separate but content instead of together and miserable. It was a concept that was hard to accept but I knew would make everything better in the long run.

Many of the girls that were at Somerset had divorced parents. It seemed to be a common theme, along with the perfectionism and people-pleasing tendencies. Once I had received news that my parents were going to be getting a divorce, I immediately began restricting what I ate. I could see the relation in my journal entries. Even though I knew that the divorce was for the better, it was still hard to accept. No one ever wants their parents to get divorced.

This pending divorce was something I couldn't control, so I began to control what I ate and started to lose all the progress I had gained. My weight dropped a few pounds. I was eating less and less and was isolating myself more and more. And with writing everything down in the journal, I could really make the connection with my feelings and food.

Once I realized this, I began talking about it in the group therapy sessions, which to my surprise, helped greatly. For the first time, I didn't feel numb. I actually felt upset. Sad. Depressed. Everyone listened to me, and most of them even related to how I was feeling. For the first time, I was now feeling normal. And for the first time, I was being myself. And I was happy about it.

And thus the roller coaster ride of recovery continued. I would take a few steps forward with a few steps back in between, but the steps forward outweighed the steps back. I was definitely making progress.

As I started to get better and eat better, I began to feel the urge to exercise. I believe that was mostly due to the physical aspect of eating again, not the emotional aspect. I was feeling full most days, and sitting around in a hospital all day didn't help. Luckily, as long as I kept gaining weight, which averaged a couple pounds a week, I was allowed off the unit for a walk, twenty minutes at a time.

Walking made me feel good, but running made me feel even better. I went from taking Diet Coke breaks with the other girls to going for runs alone, along the side streets, where I wouldn't run into any doctors or nurses. Although I didn't have the energy to do much running, nor the time since I only had twenty minutes, it still felt good to have some kind of cardiovascular activity during the day.

Sometimes my roommate Devon and I would exercise in our room as well, which was forbidden. But we figured out ways to skirt the issue. At night, when the door was shut, the video cameras could not see what we were doing. We'd do sit-ups and jumping jacks in the dark, which ended up being more fun than exercise. It was all about the thrill of doing something against the rules. And we were succeeding.

By the fourth week of my stay, I had reached ninety-nine pounds and was hoping for a weekend pass, along with Devon. Our one contingency was that we'd both have to, at a minimum, maintain our weight from Friday to Saturday. We did not want to take any chances. We wanted to get out into the real world for at least a couple hours. So we took drastic measures.

We decided to wake up at five a.m. and drink five sixteen-ounce cups of water from our bathroom sink. We needed to assure that our weight did not go down. Sure enough, we both gained a half pound and were granted six-hour passes for the day.

We could go anywhere and see anyone. The only rule was that we needed to adhere to our 1800-calorie-a-day regimen. We ate breakfast at the hospital and would eat dinner upon our return. However, we'd be eating lunch out in the real world, and we had decided to go to Chili's.

Chili's had the best salads. After much consideration, we both decided on a grilled chicken salad, with fat-free dressing on the side, of course. And to drink—well, that was an easy choice: Diet Coke, since we would never dream of drinking calories if we didn't have to. And by this point, four weeks into my treatment and four weeks with being Nutrasweet deprived, we each poured over five packets of Sweet'n-Low into our large glasses of Diet Coke. It tasted so good. This was a milestone. We were both at a restaurant eating a normal meal. I was living my dream.

This was the first time I had entered the real world after being hospitalized for weeks. I ate, voluntarily, in front of one of my peers, for the first time in a very long time, and it felt really good. It just made me want to fight my eating disorder even more.

I now desired so much to be back with my friends, getting ready to go off to college. I missed gossiping on the phone every night. I missed hanging out with my sister after school. Instead, I was cooped up in a hospital wing, twenty-four hours a day, with limited phone privileges and access to one shared TV. I felt like I was missing out on so much. I realized that I didn't want to miss out on anything more.

After our meal at Chili's, Deb and I made our way to the mall for some shopping, then to my house, then hers, and finally back to the medical center. Upon our arrival, dinner was served. It was hard coming back, but at the same time, it felt good to go back to my safe place.

Here at the hospital I had meals delivered to me, three times a day. Each portion of food was measured according to my appointed caloric intake. I had no access to junk food, which would potentially force me to binge. Here at the hospital, I was surrounded with an extremely healthy environment. As much as I looked forward to being on the outside, for now the inside was where I needed to be. The inside took a lot of stress off of eating and helped me to focus more on the other issues that I needed to deal with, but I knew eventually I could handle being on the outside. Now I was looking forward to it.

The next three weeks flew by. I had started to deal with my parents' relationship. I was coming to the realization that I didn't have to be perfect, and I was learning to do things for myself, not just for others. Everything was starting to make sense, and I was in a good place to deal with it. But I still needed to deal with the identity issue. The eating disorder had been what made me feel special all those years. Now what was I going to do without it? Well, I soon learned.

One afternoon during the last week of my stay, I sat in the common room with a few other girls while we watched General Hospital. Devon asked if I could french braid her hair and I joyfully agreed. I loved to do people's hair.

As I was finishing the braid and twisting the bottom with a rubber band, Jen (one of the four Jens on the unit) looked at the braid in amazement. She turned to me and asked, "Is there anything you can't do?"

I quickly replied, "What are you talking about?"

"You dance, play soccer, play the piano and violin, you tutor kids in math. Needlepoint. Crochet. You can do everything!" she exclaimed.

Jen was just so impressed that I could do all of these things and now, in addition, could french braid hair. She said she was so jealous of me for all of my talents.

Wow. I just sat there. Stunned. All this time, I was giving myself such a hard time for not being the best at anything. I never felt like I was special because I was never the captain of the soccer team or the solo violinist. But now, for the first time, I realized that I was special because I could do so many things, and I was pretty decent at most of them. Maybe I wasn't the best at any one, but I was good at them all. And that was great. For the first time, I felt special, and that was the greatest feeling in the world. Being Jen was a pretty good thing.

Two months and eighteen pounds later, I was released from Somerset Medical Center. I was hesitant about returning home. I had been successful at beginning the recovery process by surrounding myself in a structured environment where I felt safe. Safe to be myself. Safe to express how I felt. And safe to eat and gain weight.

Going home would be different. It would be unstructured. Food would be available at any time, not delivered on a tray at set times throughout the day. I would have to sit at the dinner table night after night while my parents watched my every bite. I would have to sit at the lunch table day after day while my friends stared in amazement, as they hadn't seen me eat normally in over a year. But at the same time, going home would make me feel normal again. How wonderful it was going to be to see my friends every day and to sleep in my own bed, in my own room, with my Tom Cruise poster over my bed. I knew it wasn't going to be easy, but this was eventually going to happen and I was as prepared as I ever would be. This was just the next step in the recovery process. I had faith.

Through the end of the school year, I attended outpatient therapy twice a week while attending school three days a week and continued with individual therapy as well. I made some adjustments in my schedule so I could ease back into a semi-normal routine.

For lunch, I would meet my friend Maggie in the guidance office and eat a frozen Carnation Instant Breakfast shake (a.k.a. CIB). The nurse let me keep my frozen CIB in her freezer throughout the morning. This was more comfortable for me rather than eating at a table with twenty people and feeling like forty eyes were on me. I also kept my daily menu to only include my "safe" foods such as cottage cheese, bananas, yogurt, cereal, and bagels. For the next few months, I ate bagels and cottage cheese for every meal. These were the only foods I was comfortable with. That was fine. At least I was eating.

The hardest part about returning to school and home were people's comments. They'd say, "Oh Jen, you look so healthy," or "Jen, you just look so much better now." These comments meant one thing to me and one thing only: I was getting fat. The fact that I was looking healthy meant that I had gained weight and therefore was not skinny anymore. This was not good. These words were hard to stomach. I'm sure that people meant these comments as compliments, but for someone who was a recovering anorexic, these were taken as insults.

But I took them in stride. Everyone else that had entered the world of an outpatient was dealing with the same issues, so we'd talk about them at group, and I realized I wasn't alone and that looking healthy was a good thing. I kept reminding myself that going to college and starting over with a new identity was my end goal.

Luckily, the summer came quickly. I attended my senior prom with my high school sweetheart. I passed my final exams and celebrated my high school graduation. Everything was going as planned.

When it was time to start a summer job, I made the decision to stick with the part-time therapy instead of working full-time. I wanted to be close to a full recovery before leaving for college, so I continued to deal with my issues and found that the road to recovery was not a straight line. There were many bumps and turns along the way and as the time approached to leave for school, I hit one major curve in the road.

I had been packing up my things for school and was exhausted, mentally and physically. Every day I was continually analyzing my every move. Analyzing my every thought. My every feeling. I was writing in a journal. Talking to therapists. Talking to my family. My friends. It was extremely overwhelming.

It was about nine o'clock at night when I finally laid down to relax. As my head hit the pillow, I immediately started to cry. All of a sudden, I just didn't want to deal with the issues anymore. It was tough. Stressful. Maybe if I could just take some pills to numb the pain. I had been numb for so long, and now all of a sudden I was feeling all of these emotions. Happiness. Sadness. Anger. Joy. Confusion. It was all just too overwhelming.

My antidepressant pills were on my nightstand just waiting for me to consume. I grabbed the little brown container, poured a bunch of the pills into my hand, tossed them into my mouth, and washed them down with a glass of water. Then I laid still. Staring at my wallpapered ceiling, counting the rows of bunched flowers, I closed my eyes and desperately tried to fall asleep just hoping the emotional pain would subside. What had I done?

Thirty minutes came and went. I couldn't stop thinking about the pills I had taken as I tossed and turned and tried to get comfortable.

"What the hell should I do?" I asked myself.

I was 99 percent sure that I would be okay. The pills would just work their way through my system and by tomorrow I would be okay. I had nothing to worry about. Well, all except for that 1 percent of doubt. It was that 1 percent of uncertainty that was keeping me awake.

"What if those pills really can kill me?" I nervously contemplated. "What if I go to sleep and I never wake up?"

Shit. The thought of that scared the shit out of me. I didn't want to die. Really, I didn't. I wanted to just go to sleep and wake up normal, with no more eating issues or emotional issues. I just wanted to be normal. Not dead.

I decided I had to go to the doctors. And I had to tell my mom. I finally worked up enough courage to tell my mother, and of course, she freaked out and immediately drove me to the emergency room. And what happened next was one of the most excruciating experiences of my life.

I was forced to drink liquid charcoal. Apparently, liquid charcoal would cause me to throw up, thus cleansing out the pills in my stomach. It was thick. It was black. It was cold. And it was gritty. It had to be the most distasteful thing I have ever had to drink in my entire life. And there was a ton of it.

It made me nauseous and made me gag. Each time I would gag, the liquid charcoal would come up through my nose and my mouth. I had black charcoal all over my face. In my nostrils. In my hair. On my neck. I couldn't get away from it. It was complete hell. I swore at that moment that I would never overdose on any medications ever again. I wouldn't even take three Advil if the normal dose was two. I could never stand to drink this liquid grit ever again.

After talking with the doctors at the ER, they let me go, seeing as that it wasn't considered attempted suicide. I claimed I just wanted to hurt myself. It was yet another way of inflicting physical pain instead of dealing with my emotions. They made me sign a waiver claiming that I would continue therapy when going off to school. I agreed. I knew I still needed help.

The first day of college finally came. After years of anticipation, I was finally moving into a dorm room at Boston College. I came to school two weeks early for dance team tryouts. Grueling workouts and practices were scheduled. It was physically challenging but a great deal of fun. I was meeting lots of great new people with every new day. It was greatly relieving to start over. I had a clean slate in front of me, and I was using it to every bit of my advantage. No one knew about my past, and I could be anyone I wanted to be. I could be the smart one or the funny one or the athletic one. I was no longer the anorexic one, which made me happy.

My biggest challenge at school was eating in front of people. Even though nobody knew about my past, I still wasn't comfortable eating most foods. I was still on my safe food diet, which consisted mostly of fruit, muffins, bagels, and frozen yogurt. It was a little embarrassing to bring a muffin and frozen yogurt to the dinner table, but I managed to make excuses.

"Oh, I had a big lunch," I would say casually, or, "I'm going to practice tonight and I can't dance on a full stomach."

After a few weeks, I began to feel more comfortable with food and tried venturing out. Sometimes I'd have a bowl of rice or a plate of vegetables. For some reason, eating protein was the hardest obstacle to overcome. For months, I would eat only carbs and veggies for my meals. My nickname even became "Side-Order Jen." But over time, I was able to work in some chicken and burgers and even desserts like cake and ice cream. And candy too. By December, I had actually started looking forward to meals. I didn't remember food tasting so good!

Eating became second nature for me over my first semester. I was so busy with schoolwork, classes, and dance team I didn't have time to count calories or worry about my meals. I was doing things that I enjoyed, like choir and volunteer work, which boosted my self-confidence. I also continued with a therapist one day a week so I could continue working through my family and personal issues. My eating disorder was beginning to feel like something of the past. I got rid of my small clothes and looked at it as an opportunity to go on a shopping spree. I bought a whole new wardrobe for the whole new me. And I went off all of my medications. Everything was going according to plan.

But then came Valentine's Day. For weeks, I had been playing phone tag with my boyfriend, but we always managed to miss each other. He was now a sophomore at Rutgers University in New Jersey, and I was up in Boston. The phone was our main source for communication. Email was still a fairly new phenomenon.

Now, since it was Valentine's Day, I expected him to make a surprise visit. Instead, I got a fucking email that wasn't even personalized to me. It was a forward about Cupid that he had gotten from somebody else. Well, I could certainly read between the lines. The relationship had finally come to an end. It wasn't a complete shock. Things had been going downhill for a while, so I was somewhat prepared, but it was still tough. He had been my first long-term relationship. There was certainly some emotional impact.

However, I tried to stay in good spirits. Spring break was only two weeks away, and I was ready to come home and visit my friends. It was my first spring break of college. I knew my parents didn't have the money to send me away on a lavish vacation, so I opted to come home for the entire week.

My mom drove up to Boston to pick me up. On our way home, she mentioned that she and my dad were officially getting a divorce. It wasn't a surprise, but it was still a huge change for us. My parents had been married for twenty-eight years. I felt especially sad for my father. He so badly wanted to stay together and make it work, but my mom knew that it would never be what she needed or expected out of a relationship, so she decided to make it official and break ties.

So I break up with my high school sweetheart and my parents file for divorce, all within a two-week period. That was a lot of bad news to handle all at once, especially without my vice. My addiction. The coping mechanism that had helped me through so much before. I was without it. I was vulnerable and had nowhere else to go, so I caved in and I went back to starving myself. I went back—kicking and screaming, but I still went back.

It started immediately when I got home. I cut back and told my mom I was still living on my safe foods. She catered to my every need and fed me bagels and cottage cheese for the week. When I returned back to school, things took a turn for the worse.

I tried to go every day as long as I could without eating a thing. I'd usually make it until mid-afternoon, and then I would end up bingeing on my roommate's food when she wasn't there. I would scarf down as much as I could, whether it be Cheez-Its or Yodels, and then I would make a run across the hall into the girls' bathroom. I would take showers and try to throw up as much as I could in the shower stall. It was less conspicuous to do it in there since the dripping water would drown out the gagging noise.

Once I was done throwing up, I would cut myself with my razor as a punishment. The cuts would remind me of the fatness I felt when I ate and would prevent me from bingeing. Some days, they worked. Some days, they didn't. Sometimes my hunger was so overpowering, I just had to eat. When it got to that point, I'd eat anything that was available. God, anything to feed my hunger. Anything to feed the pain.

This relapse lasted for about six weeks. By the middle of April, I couldn't take it anymore. I was so disappointed in myself. I remembered how happy I used to be with my friends and with myself. Now I was miserable.

Friday nights, I would lie in bed with the comforter over my head listening to "She's Got a Problem" by Fountains of Wayne on repeat while my roommate would go out with our friends. What the hell was wrong with me? Why couldn't I just talk about my issues with my friends and deal with them? I was compressing everything I was feeling and it was just so frustrating. I finally decided to call my mom and tell her what was going on. I talked to my psychiatrist from home and he re-prescribed my medication, Zoloft. I knew I was taking the right step and that I would soon be back to normal. Or so I thought.

We had one week of classes left and then finals. I was terribly upset that we were all leaving for the summer. I had fallen in love with school and wished I could stay there year-round. I didn't want to go home because my parents would be there, still living in the same house but going through the divorce proceedings. I knew it was going to be uncomfortable, but I was just going to have to deal with it and try to focus on enjoying my last few weeks of fun.

But the thought of going home, and possibly my bad habits returning, became too overwhelming. The thought of potentially killing myself consumed me. What a relief it would be if I didn't have to deal with any of this anymore. What a peaceful thought. So, long story short, I ended up overdosing again. This time, I took thirteen Zoloft.

Before I did it, I typed a letter to my friends and family on my computer. I said that I loved them and if anything happened to me, it wasn't their fault. I left this message in a text file open on the computer while it was in sleep mode. Then, I took the pills and lay on my bed. I wasn't as scared this time. I was tired and wanted to go to sleep. At one point I confessed to my roommate that I had taken a few too many pills, but I convinced her that it was no big deal and she shouldn't tell anyone. What a mistake.

I was able to fall asleep, but at seven a.m. I woke up and felt absolutely horrible. My body was shaking and I felt weak and achy. My eyesight was blurry. I felt all out of sorts. I knew that the pills were still inside my system and needed to come out.

I immediately called my therapist, who then called the campus security. Two policemen showed up and escorted me out of the dorm building. My roommate came with me and they drove us straight to the emergency room. As usual, I was hooked up to an IV and had to drink the liquid charcoal. Hadn't I just been through this? Didn't I tell myself that I would never make myself go through this torture again? Why didn't I listen to myself? This was an absolute nightmare.

To make matters worse, after they talked to my roommate, they decided to send me home from school. I was being kicked out of the last few weeks of school. They said I could come back the following year. I just couldn't stay to finish final exams. I had to go home for therapy and would need to send in my finals from home. This was devastating. I would miss all of the end-of-the-year parties and events, and I was going to have to move out of the dorm early, which meant everyone was going to know that something happened to me. So much for my secret. No more clean slate. I was yet again "the sick girl."

You've been keeping to yourself these days
Cause you're thinking everything's gone wrong
Sometimes you just want to lay down and die
That emotion can be so strong
But hold on till that old second wind comes along

–Billy Joel, "Only Human"

7 | 100% recovery: does it exist?

That final relapse was the straw that broke the camel's back. Leaving school early made me realize that my disease was preventing me from having some extremely fun experiences. I knew that I had to get better in order to enjoy life, so I fought back and won that summer. I couldn't be the sick girl anymore.

I stuck with the therapy and dealt with all of my issues and learned how to resolve them. For starters, I had to come to terms with the fact that you cannot change people. Instead, you need to learn how to change your expectations. My mother had been extremely overbearing over the years, and I finally realized she depended on my life to fulfill her own. This put a ton of pressure on me as I felt that, if I failed, I not only failed me but I failed her. Through therapy, I finally figured this out and was able to communicate to her how her actions affected me. And although I told her this, she didn't quite understand it, so her behavior never changed, but telling her still made me feel better. It made me realize that she is only worrying so much or nagging me so much because she cares, and I'm okay with that. It's better than her not caring at all.

Additionally, I accepted my father's withdrawn personality. I recognized that his actions were not so much a reflection of his feelings toward me as just his personality and what he is comfortable with. When he came home after work and sat in front of the TV set instead of eating dinner with us or coming to my school concert, it wasn't because he didn't love me. It was because he just wanted to relax and unwind. I was never going to change that. I did tell him that when he did those things, it hurt my feelings, but again, he didn't change his behavior going forward. He still did what he wanted to do and I had to accept it. I knew he still loved me. He just showed it in a different way, and I learned to live with it.

Overall, the most important lesson I learned was to communicate my feelings. Happiness. Sadness. Anxiety. Anger. Confusion. Whatever I felt needed to be communicated instead of staying bottled up inside. When people don't deal with their emotions, they cope with them in other ways, such as drugs, alcohol, and in my case, eating disorders. These are all unhealthy ways of dealing with stressors instead of dealing with them head-on.

Once I was able to start dealing with my emotions in a healthy way, my damaging coping mechanism became less and less of an issue. My body image began going back to normal as well. I ate healthy and exercised well. I spent time with both my high school friends and college friends, and I also made time for me. I made a vow to myself that I would go back to college my sophomore year and prove to everyone that I was the same girl they met first semester.

So I went back to Boston College that fall and immediately volunteered for MEDA (the Massachusetts Eating Disorder Association). I answered phone calls from friends and family of those suffering from eating disorders and gave them advice on how to handle their situation. It was a healthy way to still be involved with the anorexia. It helped me realize how great it was being healthy and how much I never wanted to go back to being sick ever again.

Sophomore year was a blast. I had a new boyfriend, who I met in New Jersey over the summer and continued to date long-distance when I went back to school. I declared my major as Psychology, as I was greatly enjoying the few psych classes that I had taken so far. I continued with the dance team and lived with my same roommate from freshman year. Everything was finally going according to plan. I was finally enjoying life just as I had hoped.

The only difficult issue that I was still dealing with was that of my parents' divorce. It was finalized that spring, and since the lawyers cost my parents close to everything they had, money was tight. My mom moved into a low-income housing unit across town with my sister, and my dad moved in with his parents just a few towns away. I knew that they really couldn't afford for me to continue at Boston College the following year, so I had two options: either transfer to a cheaper school close to home, or take out more loans and pay for it myself sometime down the road.

As much as I loved Boston, I decided that I should come home. I would not only save money but I'd also be able to be close to my parents and sister. I wanted to be near them during this tough time. They were all struggling, and I felt like the strongest one at that point. I had been through so much already but had gained so much strength because of it. They had helped me, and now it was my time to help them.

I decided to transfer to Drew University. My mother worked at Drew, which provided a discount, and I wouldn't need housing since it was so close to home. Their academic program was just as strong as BC's but had a more personal touch. Each graduating class had only three hundred students, so I would get a lot of personal attention from the professors. Although I'd miss my friends, I knew that Drew was the right choice.

Back in New Jersey, I continued with my volunteerism. Throughout my junior year, I became involved with the National Eating Disorders Association. I attended the conference for the NJ Chapter that fall and was able to meet some fellow recovered women as well as therapists. Through my new network of professionals, I helped organize panel discussions at colleges, spoke at middle schools and high schools, and even helped run support groups at hospitals.

The most common question I received at these events was "Is 100-percent recovery possible?" And my answer was yes, absolutely. I had gotten to such a happy and healthy point in my life that eating and body image were never an issue. I firmly believed that you could take control of your life and would never have to deal with the eating disorder ever again.

Seven years went by. I finished college with a degree in Psychology and got a job at an insurance company where I had interned during the summers. For years I worked my way up the ladder as a project manager, using my organizational skills to their fullest capacity. I met a man through work and fell in love. He was a wonderful, good soul. We were married by the time I was twenty-five and bought a house, an old Victorian, complete with an old English garden out back and wrap-around porch. A few months after we returned from our honeymoon, we adopted a yellow lab puppy and named her Morgan. My perfect little life was forming right before my very eyes. I had everything I had ever wanted: a good husband, a beautiful house, and a well-paying job. What more could I want?

It was now the spring of 2005. I was twenty-seven years old and miserable. As I quietly mulled over my life on my front porch, all I could think of was the distance between my husband and I. "Marriage is not supposed to be this way," I thought to myself.

Wearing my white large-brimmed hat served two purposes that afternoon: one to protect my eyes from the sun, and the other to hide the black-stained tears streaming down my face. Steve and I had only been married for a year and a half, but I already doubted our hollow relationship. Emptiness was a constant feeling for me. It seemed as though one day morphed into the next and my life was just passing me by without me really living it.

"When did things change?" I asked myself.

I desperately yearned for an answer. I was convinced that there had been some action or event that had caused our relationship to deteriorate. We rarely fought; however, we rarely had sex either. Our interactions became strictly platonic, as if we were roommates instead of a married couple. The concept of divorce briefly crossed my mind, leaving me to ponder how life as a single woman would be better than my current domesticated lifestyle. At that point, being single would be just as equally lonely.

I so desperately wanted to be understood. It was starting to become clear that my husband didn't really know who I was. Our personalities were tremendously different, often leaving me to feel alone. I tried to envision our future together and it just didn't make sense, but this was what I signed up for. This was certainly a long-term commitment that was not easy to get out of. We couldn't just break up. This would mean divorce. I just couldn't imagine going through with it.

I spent the next few months frantically trying to communicate my needs and figure out how we could make the marriage succeed. No matter what I tried, nothing seemed to work. I just didn't understand why I couldn't fix it. Steve was a great guy. Why couldn't he change? I reminded myself that you can't change people. They can change only if they want to, and if they don't, you have to learn how to deal with who they are. I could deal with Steve as a friend, but I couldn't deal with him as a husband.

By the end of the year, I had decided that divorce was the only way to go. He so desperately wanted to go to counseling and work things out, but by then it was too late. The time and energy I spent throughout the summer was the time we should have been in counseling. Now it had reached a point where my romantic feelings for him were gone. I still loved him to a great extent, but as a friend, not as a husband. Maybe that is enough to some people, but it just wasn't enough for me.

I immediately moved in with my dad, and by the spring of 2006, our house was on the market. We agreed to wait to file for the divorce until the house was sold and we could settle everything all at once. In the meantime, I began the search for a new job. I hadn't been happy with my job either and knew I needed to be doing something different, I just didn't know what that was.

I started by searching the job listings available within my company throughout their various other locations. I applied for a job at my company's home office in Connecticut and was offered the position within a week. I moved a month later. The idea of starting over was gradually becoming a reality. I was greatly looking forward to a new work environment, new social circles, new friends, new neighborhoods to explore, and most importantly, being on my own. I hadn't been single since high school, so being independent and on my own was new territory for me—one that I looked forward to but was terrified of, all at the same time. But my excitement surpassed my anxiety and I began my new life with a positive outlook.

I began adapting to my new lifestyle rather quickly. By the fall I had established a strong circle of friends, mostly from work, but it also included those from my dance class and soccer team. Additionally, I had developed a respectable reputation at the office and had even started entering the dating world. While my adjustment to the new environment was going smoothly, I was finding difficulty in achieving closure with the aspects of the life I left behind.

Our house was not selling. It had been on the market since May, and paying both rent and a mortgage every month was not an easy assignment. I was stressed out beyond belief as my credit card debt began to increase with no end in sight. We also hadn't filed for divorce yet, because our original plan was to wait until the house was sold to solidify the split. However, due to the house sale taking longer than expected, we finally decided to file for divorce in August. Unfortunately, it was estimated to take eight to nine months for finalization. Even though I desperately wanted to move on, these hindrances were delaying that process.

It had been years since I had felt this helpless and my life seemed this unmanageable. There were so many factors that I couldn't control. I couldn't make the divorce process any faster, nor could I induce the sale of the house. I felt powerless. Helpless. Here I was, twenty-eight years old, with hardly any assets, a job at which I spent eleven hours a day but wasn't passionate about, and a profound negativity surrounding my future. I was overwhelmed and beginning to feel like a failure.

So little by little, I slowly resorted back to restricting my food intake. I needed to feel in control of something in my life. Since I couldn't control these life-changing impediments, I fell back onto my once-familiar crutch where I peacefully felt in control: self-starvation. In addition to restricting my intake, I became more rigorous with my exercise regimen. I bought a scale so I could track my decrease in weight. It was happening again. Losing weight was slowly becoming an obsession.

It was now December and I had had one of those weeks that dragged on forever, but Friday night finally came. I had made plans to meet my friend Stacy for dinner at a Mexican restaurant in downtown Hartford. I was greatly looking forward to a night out with her so we could catch up. I hadn't seen her in weeks.

Unfortunately, the anxiety over what I was going to eat when I was with her was unnerving. I had the plan in my head that I could only eat a certain amount of food and it had to be healthy. If I could just stick with that plan, then maybe I would even treat myself to a margarita.

Even though the restaurant was crowded, we were able to get seated right away. At first glance, the table we got seemed to be the only empty one left. As we sat down, the waitress handed us our menus. This was uncomfortable. At this moment I couldn't even dream of opening the menu, but there it was staring at me in the face. I took a deep breath and tried to think for a moment about a time when I looked forward to going out to dinner. It wasn't even that long ago. All I wanted was to go back to that place. That comfortable, happy, non-stressful place. But I was far from it. All I could think about was how little I ate all week and the few pounds that I had already lost. I needed to keep it up. I needed to restrict as best I could. I couldn't be weak. I had to stay in control.

Stacy began to browse the menu. "Do you want to order the guacamole?" she quickly asked.

"Sure, definitely," I chirped back.

What was I thinking? That is going to be too much on top of my meal. Maybe I'd just eat the guac then. That made sense. I could just have some chips and the guac and be all set for the night.

"What are you going to get for dinner?" Stacy proceeded to inquire.

"Umm, I'm not sure yet," I answered.

Ok, how was I going to get away with this one? I know she will think it's weird if I just eat the chips. I had to get something. Maybe I would only have one or two chips and then just focus on my meal. Yes, that would certainly work. I was already feeling better. I spent the next ten minutes agonizing over my choices. What a tough decision. My heart wanted the burrito but my mind was saying salad.

I was leaning towards the salad when the waitress came back to take our order. Stacy ordered first and ordered a large chicken burrito. It sounded so good. I couldn't resist. I had to have one too. I was starving. I had lived on crackers, peanut butter, and coffee all week, so now I needed food. Real food. Food that would make me feel full. Food that would make me feel better. Food that would comfort me and make me feel complete.

Without even thinking, I ordered the burrito. A large chicken burrito with rice, cheese, and beans. Yum. Even though I was mad at myself for ordering it, I was still looking forward to inhaling it the second it arrived. I knew I had an option waiting for me at home. I'd just throw it up.

A couple weeks prior, I found a website from which I could order ipecac. It was so easy. So much easier then when I was in high school. Back then, we were supposed to be eighteen and we had to sign for it, even state a reason for buying it. In those days, I would go to a different pharmacy every time so that they wouldn't have me on record buying it twice. It was only supposed to be kept on hand for emergency situations. Wasn't eating too much an emergency situation? I thought so, so I purchased a few bottles but had yet to use them.

The guacamole arrived and I still wanted to try to limit my food intake. I tried to convince myself to plan on taking home leftovers. I didn't want to get too full, and I really didn't want to resort to the ipecac. That really was only a last resort.

I took my first chip and dipped it into the guacamole. Wow, did that taste good. I hadn't tasted anything that good in a long time. I was in heaven. Luckily, I had already finished half of my huge margarita, so my anxiety had decreased a bit. And Stacy was continually talking, so that helped distract me from thinking about what I was eating.

I had another chip. And another. And another. I finally realized that I couldn't stop. I was starting to binge. I wasn't even tasting anything that was going into my mouth at this point. It was all going down so fast. I tried to slow down a bit, but our meals appeared shortly after. I knew this was now going to be an ipecac night.

So I began to eat my burrito. I took my first bite. Yum. I think it was even better than the guacamole. I took my second bite. Yes, it was definitely better than the guacamole. There were so many textures and flavors going on at the same time. And once I started I just couldn't stop. I ate almost the entire thing before I realized that my stomach was hard as a rock. I was terribly uncomfortable, so I ordered another margarita. That would certainly make me feel better.

An hour later, the alcohol had started to wear off and I could clearly feel the large mass that had grown inside my stomach. The anxiety started to come back as we finished up our conversation. I must have started digesting some of that food by now. This was not good at all. I needed to get all of this food out of my system as fast as possible. Stacy began to appear tired, so I jumped at the chance to suggest our departure. Sure enough, she agreed.

I rushed home. All I could think about were those bottles of ipecac I so cleverly hid in my kitchen cabinet behind the peanut butter jar. I was home in fifteen minutes. I ran inside and up to my apartment. As soon as I got in the door, I went straight into the kitchen. I took out one bottle of ipecac and set it down on the counter. Was I really going to do this? Yes, of course I was. I felt so gross. All that food was making me feel so uncomfortable. I had to get it out of me. There was no other choice.

I opened the bottle. I slowly held it up to my nose in order to get a sense for what it smelled like. As I got my first whiff, the memories of high school and bingeing in my bedroom came back in an instant. It was a god-awful smell, so bad that it made me gag. I put it down and took a step back.

"Ok, now, am I really going to do this?" I anxiously questioned myself.

I had forgotten how toxic that stuff was and how difficult it was to swallow, but I just couldn't back out now. I had eaten way too much. This was my punishment. I had lost control and needed to be reprimanded. Perhaps this would prevent me from bingeing ever again.

While pinching my nose shut, I followed a swig of ipecac with half a can of diet ginger ale. Then, I slowly proceeded to release my sweaty fingers from my nostrils. Ugh. I could still taste the ipecac. The taste was horrific. Just the smell of it made me gag. Disgusting. I quickly drank the rest of the ginger ale and wiped my lips with a wet cloth. I needed all remnants of the toxic syrup to be stripped from my taste buds.

Now all I had to do was wait. I placed the bottle, now half empty, back into the kitchen cabinet, turned off the kitchen lights, and made my way into the family room. I sat down on the couch, put on my glasses, and cuddled up with a pillow placed over my stomach. Television would be the best distraction while I was anticipating the results.

About fifteen minutes later, I began to feel nauseous. "Okay, here we go," I thought to myself. I couldn't wait to get rid of all that bad food that I ate. Oh, God. I couldn't just walk up the stairs. I had to run. It was coming up fast.

Luckily, I made it to the toilet before anything came out. And boy did the food come out. It seemed like everything I had eaten that day came out of my body. Large thick chunks of food poured out of my mouth. It was so gross yet so relieving at the same time. I was draped over the toilet for what seemed to be an hour but in reality was only about two minutes.

Once the gagging sensation was gone, I gradually sat up and leaned my weak body against the wall. Tears streamed down my face, not because I was crying but from having my head tipped forward for such a long period of time. I slowly tilted my head back and closed my swollen eyes.

"What am I doing?" I asked myself.

At that moment, I knew I was at the point of no return. I was officially addicted to my eating disorder once again. It had been ten wonderful years since I had used this as my survival mechanism. I thought I would never go back to it. I was convinced that it would just never be an option again, but I was wrong. I had fallen.

I took a few deep breaths and found the strength to stand up. I rinsed my puffy red face with a cold wet washcloth and blew my nose. Okay, the worst was now over. I could relax and calmly fall asleep, knowing that all those calories I had consumed were now out of my system. I jaunted down the stairs to my couch and continued to watch reruns of *The Real World*. I drank some soda and curled up with my afghan. Boy, did I feel better.

But fifteen minutes later, my mouth began to water again. How could I get sick again? I had nothing left in my stomach, but I figured I should go back to the bathroom just in case. I went back upstairs and kneeled in front of the toilet. Waiting. Anticipating the regurgitation. Sure enough, less than a minute went by and I started heaving again. A little more food came up, followed mostly by acidic saliva. I couldn't believe how much it burned my throat and how much energy it took out of me. Was I really going to make this a routine?

In a few minutes, the heaving stopped and once again, I rinsed my face with a cold washcloth. Looking in the bathroom mirror, all I could see was someone who was scared. Scared by the present. Scared of the future. I felt as if I was losing everything and gaining nothing. I was lost. No matter how hard I tried, I couldn't grip onto anything. I felt as if I was trying to hold onto life with all the strength that I had, but my hands were still slipping. My fingers were slowly losing their grip. I honestly didn't know how much longer I could hold on.

Exhausted, I came out of the bathroom and fell into my bed. I couldn't wait to pass out and happily did in roughly fifteen seconds. Unfortunately, about a half hour later, I awoke to an intense nauseating sensation once again. My mouth was watering up. I took some deep breaths and tried to convince myself that I was not going to get sick again. I was fine. It was just a lingering feeling from before.

However, the nauseating sensation became worse, but I just couldn't summon the energy to go to the bathroom. I gagged. Saliva came out of my mouth. I turned over with my face pressing against the pillow while acidic saliva continued to pour out.

Maybe this was a dream, I thought to myself. I really wasn't getting sick. I was just imagining getting sick. Yes, that was it. It was all just a dream. So with that, I pretended like nothing was happening. I forced myself to fall back asleep with my cheek pressed upon my cold wet pillow.

The next morning I woke up with a soaking wet pillow underneath my face. I quickly sat up and began to recount the events from the night before. I knew I had gotten sick in the bathroom. I vaguely remembered getting sick there twice. At what point had I scraped myself off the bathroom floor and retreated to bed? And how did my pillow get soaking wet? Did I really drool that much?

I gave it a few seconds and the realizations finally came to me. I unpleasantly recalled the pool of saliva pouring out of my mouth during the night due to the remnants of ipecac. I had been too tired and lazy to make my way back to the bathroom. I was astonished at how many times I had gotten sick. Taking the ipecac was not as easy as I had remembered it to be and was not something I wanted to do on a regular basis, that was for damn certain.

Unfortunately, the cons of taking the ipecac did not outweigh my need to overindulge, and therefore, my struggle with bingeing continued. My second gorge-fest took place just five days later. I was driving home from dance class and I had only eaten crackers and yogurt all day. I anxiously tried to decide what I wanted to eat and all I could think of was fast food and chocolate cake.

So my first stop was the McDonald's drive-thru, where I bought a quarter-pounder with cheese and a large container of fries. Next, I ran into the Stop and Shop Supermarket for an Entimen's chocolate cake. Twenty minutes later I arrived back at my apartment, burger and cake in hand. The fries were already eaten. Within the next five minutes I finished the rest of the food, but shortly thereafter, thanks to the ipecac, it was already out of my system.

A couple of days later, I repeated the same process. On my way home from work, I bought a large pizza from Pizza Hut and a Reese's Pieces sundae from Friendly's. I ate half the pizza and all of the ice cream. Once again, the food only stayed in my system for ten minutes or so. I went through my routine and passed out in my bed only to wake up on yet another wet pillowcase.

The holidays depressed me. It was my first Christmas in years that I wasn't in my own house and hosting Christmas day with my family. I was now spending Christmas back in NJ at a local diner and movie theater with only my father. What a difference a year makes, that's all I have to say. I was lonely and deeply depressed. Needless to say, my ipecac use became somewhat of a regular occurrence. I quickly ran out of my initial supply, so I purchased more from the internet. Thank God there was easy access.

As much as I hated going through the process, I knew it would only help me achieve my goal. I wanted to weigh less than a hundred pounds like I did in high school. I had already lost seven pounds. It felt so good to be in control. I got such a rush every time I stepped onto the scale and saw the numbers getting smaller and smaller. These days, it seemed like it was the only thing putting a smile on my face.

When I got back to CT after New Years, I made plans with my cousin Rick for a mid-January visit. The day after he arrived, we decided to see a movie, and at the time, *Alpha Dogs* was the best choice.

The movie certainly captured my attention; the drama and suspense were continuous throughout the film. However, one scene in particular made a huge impression. Just towards the end, there was a scene that featured Sharon Stone, a mother of a murdered child, being interviewed at a psychiatric hospital. Her character, obviously going through great turmoil, sobbed about her desperate attempt at suicide. She had failed at her attempt simply because she had slit her wrists in the wrong direction. She had made her cuts horizontally instead of vertically.

Right at that moment, memories of cutting flooded my mind. I vaguely remembered how freeing it felt to cut. How cutting caused physical pain but rid the emotional pain. Maybe I should start cutting again, I thought. Maybe I'll even get lucky and slit my wrists the proper way. Then I wouldn't have to deal with all my crap any longer. Anything was better than dealing with my life at this point.

That Sunday night, after Rick had left, I took one of my disposable razors and broke off the blade. I bent it so that the sharp edge was sticking straight out. Next, I gathered some cotton pads and Band-Aids and finally tucked myself into bed. I was more than ready to feel some pain. I had been numb for some time.

Beneath the dull light given off by my bedside table lamp, I held the blade to the inside of my left wrist. Slowly and without hesitation, I began to slice my skin in a vertical direction. From my wrist towards the inside of my elbow, just about five inches total. It immediately stung, but I had yet to draw blood. So I did it again. And again. And again.

The more I cut, the more power I felt. The more pain was released. So I continued. It began to bleed, but I still kept going. I needed all of my pain to disappear. With each cut came a burning sensation, but also with each cut came relief. Finally, the bleeding became unmanageable and I decided to stop. I had achieved my goal. At that moment, I had completely forgotten about all my problems. There were no more emotional conflicts. My arm was no longer throbbing in agony. I was yet again numb. And surrounded by silence.

I laid there in bed a few more minutes, staring at my arm. I pressed a few cotton pads against the cuts to stop the bleeding. I felt unusually calm. And, honestly, somewhat disappointed.

Part of me had hoped that I would have had the strength to cut deep enough. Deep enough to end my life. That would have made everything so much easier. But I couldn't do it. I didn't quite have the strength. I turned off the light and pulled the covers up over my head. Maybe someday I would have the courage. Just maybe.

I barely ate anything over the next few days. All I could think about was cutting and how good it felt to release the pain. I continued to cut my wrist each night before I went to bed. Each time I tried harder and harder to break through the veins. I had reached the point where dying was a very peaceful thought. Life had become too overwhelming for me at this point. If I could just slice a little harder, I wouldn't have to deal with the job, the divorce, and the mortgage any longer. Instead, I would be free. But night after night, I somehow continued to be unsuccessful.

By Wednesday, my arm was covered with cuts but I was determined to continue my nightly routine. I had no choice but to cut through the existing wounds. Slice after slice after slice. I continued for three minutes straight. Blood was dripping down towards the inside of my elbow and I let it continue to drip off onto the sheets. I just didn't want to stop. I was hoping I could go through with it this time. I was hoping I could press deep enough. Deep enough to make me free.

While the blood continued to trickle down my arm, tears began to flow down my face. What was I doing? Did I really want to go through with this?

No, I didn't. But at the same time, I didn't know how to stop either. Why was I doing this? Why couldn't I stop? I couldn't figure it out. All I knew was that I was exhausted and lonely and afraid. And I knew, at that moment, that I desperately needed help.

I dropped the razor. I picked up a wad of tissues and pressed them up against the cuts. I cuddled up into the fetal position, keeping pressure on my wrist, and continued to sob myself to sleep. If I didn't bleed to death tonight, something would need to be done. I just couldn't go on like this anymore.

I woke up the next morning with bloody tissues dispersed across the comforter. Staring up at the ceiling, I pondered how I was going to get through yet another day. I knew I needed serious help. Going to my therapist once every other week just wasn't cutting it. I needed to take more serious action.

During my drive into work, I called my therapist Dina and left her a frantic voicemail. Within an hour, she called me back and we scheduled an emergency appointment for one thirty that afternoon. As soon as my session started, I admitted to the cutting and how I didn't know how to stop myself. There was definitely a part of me that wanted to successfully slit my wrists, and that scared me shitless. What could I do to stop this insanity?

Dina immediately suggested that I admit myself to the hospital, a psychiatric hospital in downtown Hartford. If I couldn't trust myself to be alone, then I needed to be supervised 24/7. No question. And I agreed. If this is what it was going to take, then I would try it. I would try anything at this point.

After the appointment, I drove straight home to start making the arrangements. On my way, I called Stacy to tell her about my dilemma. Luckily, she was extremely supportive.

"Don't worry about work or your family or friends. You've got to take care of yourself," she reminded me.

And she was right. As much as I was freaking out about work and what people were going to think, I needed to really focus on my own well-being. If I didn't get the help I needed, it would hurt everyone.

As soon as I got home, I called the hospital. A monotone woman with a heavy Spanish accent answered the phone. She asked me a series of questions regarding my suicidal thoughts, depression, and eating habits. I wasn't convinced that I was suicidal, and apparently, neither was she. Since my main motivator for the cutting was to feel pain, she did not automatically categorize me as suicidal. Therefore, admittance to the hospital was not necessary.

I got off the phone feeling a bit uneasy. According to the so-called experts, I didn't have to go into the hospital, which, don't get me wrong, was a good thing. Additionally, I didn't have to take short-term disability at work. So, in one sense, I was relieved. But at the same time, I was scared.

Was I really okay to be on my own? A huge part of me believed that I would never intentionally kill myself, but a small part of me knew that there was definitely a possibility. I just had to think positive and increase my therapy sessions to at least once a week, if not twice. I really needed to figure out what was going on inside that little head of mine.

I sat for a minute, contemplating my next move. Frozen still, I stared at the wall, thinking that I needed to get out of my apartment. I needed to be around people. So I called Stacy back and she immediately brought a smile to my face.

"Yes, please come on over. We'll cook dinner together. We need to celebrate Jen not going to the funny farm!" she exclaimed after I told her the news. It certainly was something to celebrate. I was going to be ok. I just knew it. No funny farm for me.

But once again, a heavy wave of anxiety came over me while driving over to Stacy's apartment. The anticipation of eating dinner was making my head spin. I had barely eaten anything in the last few weeks, and when I had splurged on normal serving sizes, it usually was followed by a swig of ipecac. But

I wanted to try. I knew I needed to try to eat a slice or two. I needed to get back to my normal, non-calorie-counting self.

Stacy had decided to make her own pizza and had just started the process when I arrived. Since the preparation took awhile, I had some time to drink a glass of wine and reach a relaxing state prior to sitting down at the dinner table. This was going to be okay, I thought to myself. I can do this.

Surprisingly, I ate two and a half pieces of pizza and was comfortable, physically and emotionally. I felt full but not too full. And I was calm. Eerily calm. I was finally ready to turn my life around. And this was just the beginning. I could tell that being around good friends was the best way to get healthy.

For the rest of the evening, we watched TV and relaxed on the couch. Part of me wanted to talk about the cutting I had done the night before, but the other part was too ashamed and was glad we had the TV as a distraction. Chances were, she wouldn't understand anyway.

However, once our regular prime-time shows were over, Stacy started probing for more information about how I had gotten to this point. I immediately released the secrets I had been bottling up inside for months. The starving, the bingeing, the purging, the crying, and yes, even the cutting. "When I try to eat normally, I can't stop and I'll end up overeating," I sobbed. "Then the guilt immediately sets in and I either race to the bathroom so I can stick my finger down my throat or I do this." As I pushed my sweater sleeve back, the six-inch-long slices on my wrist were revealed.

The tears in my eyes overwhelmed my ability to see Stacy's full reaction. I knew that this would be it. I was talking about the issues and admitting to my pain. I was finally free. She hugged me tight, side by side on the couch, wrapped tightly underneath an afghan. She hugged and I cried. It was just what I needed.

Over the next few weeks, I began to open up to my friends in Connecticut. I had felt such relief from telling Stacy about my fears; I knew that I should open up to others in order to let go more of my pain and to have more of those I could lean on during this difficult time.

I spent an hour over coffee with my boss and admitted to him that I may end up spending some time in the hospital. I wasn't sure at that point, but I was definitely going to need more time with my therapist. I needed to focus on dealing with my issues instead of just compressing them inside.

I also spoke to my friend Cindy about everything. I told her about my eating disorder in high school and how the symptoms were returning, slowly but surely. I told her that I just needed to be in control of something since I didn't feel like I had any control over anything else. I was alone. My job was overwhelming. The house wasn't selling. My bills were piling up. And I could not get a court date for the divorce hearing, which was the biggest hurdle that was keeping me from moving on. I so badly needed closure in order to move on.

But I realized that while I was waiting for my closure, I needed to lean on people. That became overwhelmingly clear. So I leaned. And I leaned hard, especially on the few in Connecticut that I had become close to. They were the ones that were the closest to my day-to-day routine. They were the ones that could see when I was down and could rejoice when I was happy. They knew me, inside and out.

When your day is long, and the night
And the night is yours alone
When you're sure you've had enough
Of this life to hang on
Don't let yourself go
Cause everybody cries
Everybody hurts, sometimes

–REM, "Everybody Hurts"

8 | everybody hurts

Valentine's day was slowly approaching. I had made plans for that evening with a girlfriend whose husband was going to be out of town. We had it all planned. Dinner. Movies. Chocolate. What more could a girl ask for? I was actually excited about it. I needed a Valentine's Day where I was single. I hadn't had one since I was fifteen. I needed to celebrate the love of not only a significant other, but the love of my friends and family and, mostly importantly, the love and acceptance that I had for myself. Yes, this Valentine's Day was going to be a momentous occasion. I just knew it.

On the day before Valentine's Day came threats of a major snow storm. And not just during the night and into the morning. It was a storm that was supposed to last for over twenty-four hours, beginning early morning and going all through the day and night. Therefore, I was expecting to not only work from home on Valentine's Day, but to miss my plans with my friend and stay home by myself instead, which was okay. It would be hard and I would be disappointed, but deep down I knew it would be okay.

I brought my laptop home with me, expecting the storm to prevent my commute the following day. Sure enough, the snow began during the night, and I woke up to a blanket of white covering the parking lot. Although the snow had ceased by the time of the morning commute, sleet had taken over and thus made the commute ten times worse. There was no way I was going to drive into work, over a half hour away. Luckily, I had my laptop at home, so I plugged it in and prepared for the long day ahead of me.

All alone on Valentine's Day. Not only would I be alone that night, but I was going to be alone all day long as well. "Lucky me," I thought to myself. I had to treat it just like a normal work day. I certainly had enough tasks to keep me busy, so I was just going to have to focus—which I was surprisingly able to do. Successfully.

I got so much accomplished that day. I even took a break and made it over to the gym for a quick workout. And when I got back home, I took a nice long soothing bath. I was going to be okay, I told myself. I was certainly going to be okay. I was strong. I knew that I was strong. I just had to see it to believe it.

That night, I bought myself some sushi and cuddled up on the couch with a glass of champagne. I made a toast to myself. I was a great person, and I needed to recognize it and celebrate it. So I did. And it was a great feeling.

A few days later, my cousin Rick came back to Connecticut to pick me up for a ski weekend in Vermont. We'd be meeting up with some of my friends from high school who I hadn't seen in years. I was ecstatic. Getting away for a long weekend was just what I needed. Work had become incredibly overwhelming, not to mention the ego-crushing personal situations I had going for me. A weekend of fun was going to be the perfect remedy for my sad soul. The perfect way to lift my spirits and rejuvenate.

The weekend was awesome. We played games, ate great food, drank really good wine, and skied at Killington, one of the best ski resorts on the East Coast. What more could one ask for?

Although I was having a blast, I couldn't help but worry about life. I had so much on my plate at work and so little time to accomplish it all. I still didn't have a date for the divorce and our house was still on the market, which meant I was paying for a mortgage that wasn't supplying any value. These were certainly not positive situations, but it was life. I needed to deal with it. I needed to find the strength to confront these issues and move in a positive direction, and I always thought that I had that strength. Until Sunday.

The ride home from Vermont was silent. I didn't really have much to say. All I kept thinking about was work and money and being alone. Any negative aspect of my life was now at the forefront of my mind, and the thought of dealing with them for much longer was just not an option. I was finally officially giving up. "Universe, you win. I'm just not strong enough to handle life anymore," I calmly told myself. I needed to end my life. It was that simple. I was too weak to continue.

So I made a plan. After I got home that Sunday afternoon, I put on my favorite outfit—jeans and a white T-shirt. I was comfortable, and I always found myself to be happy when I was comfortable. Next, I took out a good bottle of red wine. If this was going to be my last glass of wine, it needed to be good wine. Nothing but the best on the day of my suicide.

Once I had my bottle of wine on my bedside table, I rummaged through my medicine basket to find my prescription sleeping pills. I dumped them out on the counter to see how many I actually had. Twenty pills remained. "I think that will be enough," I pondered.

Between the pills and the wine, I should be sound asleep for good, which was all that I wanted at that point. I just wanted to fall asleep and never wake up. I never wanted to deal with mortgages or finances or work or family ever again. Life was just too difficult for me to have a handle on.

Next, I needed to cover my tracks. I knew my boss and my colleagues would be expecting me at work Monday morning, so I called my boss's voicemail and left a casual message stating that I would not be in. I mentioned that I desperately needed to take my car in for an oil change and also needed to get some stuff done around my apartment.

"That was convincing," I thought to myself as I hung up the phone. Why wouldn't it be? Everyone has crap that they need to take care of at some point or another. Some people take days off and call them mental health days in order to rest and rejuvenate. This would certainly give new meaning to the term "mental health day," for sure.

At this point, I knew there was no turning back. I was no longer in a stable state of mind where I was capable of reaching out for help. I was determined to take my life. The thought of never waking up was so peaceful. I was certainly ready. There was no turning back now.

I took my first few sips of wine, which ensured a steady wave of calmness. Taking a few pills into my hand and shoving them down my throat was suddenly an easy task. I quickly followed it up with another swig of wine. No worries. Completely relaxed.

To enhance the mood even further, I turned on my iPod and started playing "Everybody Hurts" by REM. "Too uplifting," I thought to myself. I needed something that defined the moment. The Frey immediately came to mind, and with that, "How to Save a Life" became the song of the night. It was perfect. As I listened to it on repeat, as I did to most songs, I wrote in my journal.

"I don't know if I want to die. I would feel free, but I would greatly upset my parents and family and friends," I scribbled.

While I wrote and drank wine, I occasionally would take breaks to cut myself. I would cut until I bled heavily, enough to wipe it across the pages of my journal. I felt the need to show the world just how much pain I was really in.

The next page continued, "Dying would be so much easier. I am weak, not strong...I think this is the end. I have no more energy for life."

Diary Entry: 2/18/07, 6:32 p.m.

Okay. All I have thought about today is suicide and how much peace that it would bring me. Ultimately, I just don't think I can handle pain. I am not strong enough. I do think that I have a good outlook on life and that the failures make the successes that much sweeter, etc. However, I have endured way too much pain over the last year and a half and not enough happiness to outweigh it.

First, there was the divorce—the emptiness of my marriage and the decision to end it. Then, the loss of my best friend. And lastly came the lonliness of the dating world. And this is all just in my personal life.

On top of all this, my self-confidence at work has decreased dramatically. My responsibilities have decreased, but my workload has increased and I am just way too overwhelmed. I feel like I have tried to express my concerns over my job but they are not being listened to.

In order to rectify the situation, I have tried to reach out to my old boss to see if I can return, but there doesn't seem to be any real desire or need from his end. So yet again, I feel nothing but rejection.

All I want to do now is give up. I know that my mom will be okay—she has Ken to take care of her. My sister will be okay because she has Dylan. My dad is the only one I worry about—I can't figure out if he is going to be okay. I hope so. He does have family, but they live a few states away. But at this point, I just can't worry about it. I need to worry about myself. So, with that being said, here is my final goodbye.

To Whom It May Concern: If I do not make it, I took twenty pills, which equates to 1000 mg of Trazadone. If I am meant to live,

I will just sleep for a long time and then wake up okay. If not, then it was just my time to go. And I am okay with that."

I continued with thoughts about dying and how at peace I was with that decision. My calmness was reflected in my writings. One could see that I wasn't afraid to pass on. I was completely prepared.

I even wrote a list of all my friends and family members that should be notified once I was found. Next to each person were their phone numbers and a little blurb about what they meant to me. I was secretly hoping that those thoughts would be read at my funeral. I wanted everyone to know that they were all wonderfully supportive people and that none of them did anything wrong to cause my death. I was my own worst enemy.

A couple of hours went by. Every fifteen minutes or so I would pop a few more pills and chase them down with red wine. By eight p.m., I was feeling very sleepy. By that point, I had swallowed all the pills and drank half of the bottle. I had also gone through two *US Weekly* magazines and a *Martha Stewart Living* magazine, which I had thrown down at the end of my bed.

Around eight twenty, I finally passed out to the faint crooning of the Frey, streaming from my iPod. "...if I stayed up with you all night then I'd know how to save a life." The funny thing was absolutely no one could have saved me at that point. No one.

Two hours later, I woke up to the rapid beating of my heart. It felt like it was going to jump right out of my chest. My iPod earphones were adding to my discomfort, so I immediately yanked them out and threw the iPod on the ground. My lips were dry and it felt like there were a handful of cotton balls in my mouth.

"Why am I awake? And how am I not dead yet?" I thought to myself.

Maybe this was the end of the road. It had to be. My heart was racing. I could hear it, and it just kept getting faster and faster. I just knew it. This was going to be the end.

"Okay, don't be scared now," I reminded myself. "It's gonna beat faster and faster until it finally gives out and stops. It's not going to hurt. You'll be fine. Just relax. You'll be fine."

Dying was such a peaceful thought at that point, especially since I felt so physically ill in additional to the mental and emotional torture I was experiencing.

I stared at the ceiling and prayed to God my heart would just stop, but it wouldn't. It kept going and going and getting faster and faster. Additionally, I was beginning to sweat and get the chills. I was not comfortable at all.

"What happened to the calm, peaceful slumber that I was hoping for?" I questioned.

This was not what I imagined. At this point, I had two options: one, wait it out, feel like crap, and hope that eventually I could fall back to sleep; or two, I could call 9-1-1.

Option two was not something that I really wanted to do. That would mean I'd be giving up. And not only that, I'd have to suffer the consequences of my actions. I'd have to miss work. I'd still have to deal with all the stresses in my life. Plus, I would now have to cope with these repercussions as well. Was it really worth it?

After about an hour of strenuous mental debate, I finally gave in. I picked up my cell phone to make the 9-1-1 call. I flipped open the phone and glanced at the tiny keypad. I could not make out any of the numbers. The keypad was entirely blurry.

"I must be going blind," I assumed.

This was serious. My vision was completely distorted. Fortunately, by using the raised dot on the 5 button, I was able to figure out how to dial 9-1-1. The dispatcher picked up. It was a young gentleman who spoke very calmly.

"Hello, what is your name? And what is your emergency this evening?" he asked.

"Um, Jennifer Devlin. I think I took too many pills," I barely muttered.

It took extreme exertion just to move my lips. I was completely drained of energy.

"Ok, what did you take?" he coolly inquired.

I tried to explain but my mind felt like mush. All I knew at that point was that I could barely move, and yet my heart was beating faster than it had ever been before.

"Please come help me," I mumbled. I wanted someone to come and take care of me. I wanted someone to make all of the pain go away.

He asked if I was alone or if there was someone with me. Unfortunately, I was all by myself. And none of my friends lived even remotely close by, where I could call them for help.

He then asked if I could get myself to the door. I honestly didn't know if I could. I pushed myself out of bed and onto the floor. My body lay still as if I were paralyzed. At that point, I thought I actually may even be paralyzed. I was scared shitless.

The dispatcher kept talking to me. "Try to move yourself towards the door. Are you on the same floor as the door?" he asked gently.

"No, I'm upstairs. The entrance to my apartment is on the first floor," I replied.

Crap, I thought. This was going to be difficult. But there was no way in hell I was going to need the emergency team to break down the door. I was going to open it, even if it killed me.

The dispatcher continued the conversation. I tried with all my might to bend my legs and crawl my way across the floor to the stairs. A few minutes later, I had made it.

"Do you think you can make it down the stairs by yourself?" he questioned.

Again, I didn't really know if I could. My entire body was moving in slow motion. It seemed like my mind was giving my body instructions, my muscles had to process them, and then, one at a time, they would work together to create a movement. It was crazy and unreal.

I pushed my butt down each stair, one by one, until I got to the bottom. What a relief. I realized at that point I could make it to the door.

"Do you want me to stay on the phone with you until the rescue squad arrives?" he asked.

"Yes, please. Yes," I stuttered. "I can't really talk back, but it's good to hear a voice while I'm waiting. Please talk to me," I requested.

I really couldn't talk. My whole face was numb. My jaw felt glued shut.

"Breathe. Just breathe," I reminded myself. That's all I could do at that point.

Slowly, I made my way to the door and hoisted myself up onto my knees so I could reach the door knob. The door auto-locked from the inside, so I had to prop it open for the emergency crew. While the door was opening, I reached for my doorstop and shoved it in the doorjamb. Immediately, I felt a sense of relief. All I had to do now was wait.

I could hear voices. Deep voices. The hallway door slammed and the voices suddenly became clear. I could hear footsteps coming towards my door. And suddenly, two brawny policemen came into my blurry view.

"Hey, what's going on?" the policeman cheerfully asked. I think he was trying to lighten the mood. Given the situation, he didn't need to try very hard.

At this point, the dispatcher on the phone told me he was going to hang up since help had arrived. As soon as I put the phone down, one of the policemen picked it up and handed it to the other man.

"What made you take all those pills?" the same man asked.

I could feel myself trying to talk, but my jaw just wouldn't move.

"I don't know," I stuttered. I knew my lips were moving, but it was so hard to maneuver my mouth. It honestly felt like my whole body had turned off. Could I potentially be paralyzed from this? I was freaking out.

The second police officer had wandered upstairs, most likely going through the scene of the crime. Meanwhile, cop number one continued to press me for information.

"Are you going through a tough time or something? You going through a divorce or a bad breakup maybe?" he suggested with his strong Boston accent.

Again, I couldn't speak, so I just nodded affirmatively.

"Yeah, I hear ya. Trust me," he stated. "I can certainly relate."

I somehow managed a giggle.

"Divorces suck," he continued.

Amen to that, I thought. I continued to laugh.

"We just need to wait for the ambulance to get here and then we're going to get you to the hospital," he affirmed. "Don't you worry. You're going to be just fine."

Meanwhile, policeman number two was still combing my apartment. I continued to lie still, staring up at the wooden ceiling planks.

Finally, after what seemed like an eternity, the rescue squad arrived. I could hear something rolling down the hallway and assumed it was the ambulance bed. I couldn't wait for someone to make me feel better. I was utterly uncomfortable.

Without hesitation, the chatty policeman took a few steps back while the rescue team entered my apartment, picked me up, and lifted me onto the mobile bed. I could barely make out any of the faces given that my vision continued to be completely blurred. I finally gave up and closed my eyes, hoping I would just fall asleep. Maybe then I'd wake up to find out this was all a bad dream. A very dreadful dream.

When I did eventually wake up, I was lying in a hospital bed with a million little attachments hooked up to me. The tiny grey room was filled with little TV screens everywhere. Beeping sounds were transpiring all around me. I had no idea where I was and why I was there.

A bluish-grey plaid curtain hung to my left, surrounding almost three quarters of my bed. My vision was still blurry, preventing me from being able to make out the individuals standing in the nurses' station. I shut my eyes and tried falling back asleep, but suddenly a burst of sickness came over me. My body froze up while my forehead began to sweat. "Oh God," I thought to myself. I was gonna puke. I quickly turned to the side of my bed and proceeded to upchuck all over the floor.

Now I finally realized where I was and why, and I had never felt that horrible in my entire life. My entire body was nearly immobile; it was like having a bad flu, with little ability to walk or see.

A nurse finally made it over to clean the floor and to ask how I was doing. I tried to talk but my jaw was still completely numb, so simple mumbling had to make do. I tried explaining how I felt as best I could—the blurry vision, the numbness, and the nausea. I was just so uncomfortable. It was unbearable.

Regrettably, she said I would have to wait a little bit longer for the doctor to come by and check my status. Then they would decide how to proceed with my treatments. A few minutes later, the doctor did show up and made the assessment that I would not need to drink charcoal or have my stomach pumped. He said it was best for me to just wait for the medication to work its way out of my system.

Normally, not having to drink liquid charcoal would have been a plus. However, at this moment, I knew that it would most likely make me feel better. It would certainly make me feel better faster than just waiting around for the meds to go through my system, yet I was in no position to argue. At that point, I just wanted to fall back asleep and wake up feeling normal. Please let that happen, I prayed. I just wanted this day to be over with.

Unfortunately, a few minutes later I realized I had to pee. There was no way I could fall back asleep while having to pee that badly, but I knew that going to the bathroom was going to be a chore and my body really wasn't up for it. Yet, I had no choice. When you gotta go, you gotta go.

I used my buzzer to grab the nurse's attention and she quickly made her way back over to my bed.

"I need to use the restroom," I muttered.

"Ok," she said. "Do you think you can make it on your own, or do you need help?"

That was a pretty dumb question, I thought to myself. "Yeah, I need help for sure," I managed to whisper. "I don't have much energy."

With that, she pressed her hand against my back to help me sit up and then pulled my legs around so that they were hanging off the edge of the bed.

"Ok, are you ready?" she questioned.

As ready as I'll ever be, I thought. This was going to be an interesting venture. I was freezing. My body was aching. I was sweating and I could barely see a thing. How was I going to do this?

I put my arm around the nurse's neck while I pulled myself up off the bed. I certainly could not stand on my own. Most of my body weight was held up by her broad shoulders as she tried to escort me around the corner and into the bathroom.

Luckily, she had put hospital socks with rubber soles on my feet, so there was little chance for me to slip on the cold tile floor. We finally made it to the toilet and I was finally at a point where I could stand on my own. She asked if I needed her assistance, but I declined.

"Just stand outside the door if you don't mind," I requested. "And keep the door open."

Dammit. The minute I sat down I noticed that I had just started my period. "Really? Seriously? Could this night get any more difficult?" I pondered.

I couldn't believe it. This was just what I needed. I could barely function, and now I was going to have to worry about this too? What a fucking nightmare. I yelled through the bathroom door asking for a maxi pad. It could not get much worse than this.

The nurse finally scurried back in what felt like a lifetime to give me a bunch of feminine products. She dropped them off but quickly returned to the nursing station to give me my privacy. However, by this point, all of the energy that I had mustered up had been drained. I could no longer sit up on my own. Cold sweats became stronger and I knew that if I didn't lie down soon, I was going to faint.

I quickly attempted to make my way back to my bed, but I soon realized I was going to collapse. In a panic, I called again for the nurse, whose attentiveness was flawless. She sprang to my side and allowed me to sprawl over her back as she returned me to the hospital bed.

Once I arrived, I swiftly crawled back into the fetal position and tried focusing on falling back asleep. I didn't want to go anywhere for a long time. I felt like shit. My heart was still racing. I was sweating. I was freezing. I was nauseous. And to top it all off, I was alone. It was absolutely the worst feeling in the world.

Hours later, I awoke in a new location. I was still in the ER, but in a smaller, more private area with less equipment and less light.

"Good morning, sleepyhead. Glad you're finally joining us today," a new nurse announced as she entered my room from behind the blue- and red-checked curtain.

"I'm Chanice," she said with a smile. "I wanted the social worker to meet with you earlier this morning, but I didn't want to wake you. Now that you're up, I'll see if she's available."

Shit. The questioning was about to begin. I was going to have to relive the previous night, which was still fuzzy, detail for every painful detail.

Less than five minutes had gone by and another new person was already in my room. It was the social worker that Chanice had mentioned. She asked for my background and I quickly gave her the Jen 101 overview. I had told it to what felt like thousands at this point so it was effortless. By all means, I had the damn speech memorized.

Once I was finally finished with giving her my background, we moved on to the tough questions.

"What were you thinking as you were taking the pills?" she asked.

I timidly responded, "Well, I had gotten to a place where life had become much too overwhelming. The thought of taking some pills and dying in my sleep became a peaceful thought in my mind. I was at a point where dying didn't scare me anymore. Living was what scared me. As I took the pills, I was sad, but not because I thought I was going to die. I was sad because I knew I was going to disappoint many people, especially my mom."

At that point, she interrupted me. "So, you were taking the pills with the expectation that you were going to die. Not just, let's say, to hurt yourself or make yourself sick," she said, trying to confirm my actions.

"Yes," I said. "Yes, I was hoping with 100 percent certainty that I would not wake up."

"Well then," she whispered, "we have to keep you here. We can't let you go back home."

"I know," I calmly replied. "I know."

I held back the tears as I imagined the panic in my mother's voice when the doctor or I would call her to tell her the news. Deep in my heart, I knew that staying in the hospital was the right thing, even though the thought of it was causing additional stress. A million things that I needed to do began running through my head, starting with the meetings that I was missing that very moment.

What would I tell work? How long would I be out of the office? When was I going to tell my mother? Should I even tell her to begin with? This was not going to be easy.

"So, how long are you going to keep me here?" I inquired. "I really can't afford to stay too long."

"Well, that all depends," she countered. "Typically, you could stay anywhere from a few days to a week or longer. It all hinges on your mental stability. We just want to make sure that when we send you home you are not going to be in a place where you would want to try this again."

Point taken. I'm not sure how they would really know that, but I'd play by their rules. They obviously had a better handle on things then I did at this point, that's for sure. She then went on to explain the admittance process and told me she'd come back with more details on the timing, the facility, and who my doctors would be. I needed to come up with a good story for my coworkers and fast. There was no way I was going to tell them that I was in a psychiatric facility that week. No way, no how.

Shortly after the social worker left my room, the other nurse returned with some random hospital food which included a cold grilled cheese sandwich, mushy french fries, and a cup of vegetable soup that was way too hot to consume. Although my selections were less than appetizing, I was starving. I had no choice but to scarf down most of the sandwich and fries. Once I had enough, I quickly proceeded to go back to sleep. Those pills were still very much active in my system. Drowsy was certainly an understatement based on my current condition.

Hours later, once again, I awoke to the nurse moving me to another new location. Apparently, I had to give up my secluded room to a new patient, and for some reason, the only place they had for me was the busy hallway of the ER.

At this point, I had slept for most of the day, and when I wasn't sleeping, I was just lying in bed thinking about how depressing my life was. I was actually fine with my new location. I was looking forward to some distractions.

Lucky for me, the new patient that was taking over my room was able to provide ample entertainment. As the emergency crew rolled in his stretcher, the oversized middle-aged man began singing the entire Grease soundtrack. I'm pretty sure it was safe to assume that he was heavily medicated. Even from back in the secluded room, I could clearly hear him and his strange requests. For starters, he demanded that one of the nurses bring him peanut butter and jelly on a wrap "to go." This was going to get interesting.

While his antics continued, I started making a mental list of people I needed to call and things I needed them to do. For starters, I knew I had to call John. He was my boss, and even though I had called out sick the day prior, I knew that he would be suspicious and would be wondering if I was really okay. Plus, now that I was going to be out of the office for an unknown period of time, he would have to know where I was and would have to inform the rest of the department.

Ugh. How I dreaded the phone call. I knew there'd be disappointment on the other end of the phone. Actually, there would be disappointment on both sides. I had really let myself down.

Once one of the nurses made her way over in my direction, I requested to use their house phone. She gladly retrieved the cordless phone and brought it over for me to use.

"No long-distance calls. Got it, hun?" she declared.

"Yes, of course," I quickly responded.

No worries there, I thought. I definitely was not planning on calling my mom—or anyone else out of state for that matter. I was going to call my boss, and that was it for now. It was three p.m. With sweaty and shaky hands, I quickly dialed his number.

"Hello, this is John," he answered.

"Hey, it's me," I retorted.

"Hey, ah, how are ya?" he asked.

"Not so good," I said. "I could be better."

"That's what I figured," he continued. "Your message didn't sound too good yesterday. Where are you?"

"I'm at Manchester Hospital," I whispered.

"Oh yeah?" he replied. "Did you do something stupid?" he questioned, knowing full well that I hadn't been in a great state of mind over the past few months.

"Yes," I reluctantly agreed.

I then went on to explain that I had taken the pills and drank the wine and that I had done it fully expecting to not be alive the following morning. I simply told him that I was just way too overwhelmed with everything going on in my life. I just couldn't handle it anymore.

He held no judgment, which was nice to find. He asked me what I needed, and I told him that all I really needed at that point was someone to go over to my apartment and bring me clothes. He said he would call our mutual friend Cindy, assuming that was okay with me.

I thought about it for a brief second, and as much as I didn't want to admit defeat to anyone else, I knew that I needed help. I was going to need a lot of help from a lot of different people. I was finally going to have to lean on my friends and family if I really wanted to get through this alive. I agreed to let him call Cindy.

In fact, I asked if he could have her call me back, and I gave him the number as it read on the cordless. I told him I was worried about what to tell everyone else at work, but he said not to worry about it. He'd think of something. And I believed him. I knew he would.

About twenty minutes later, the phone rang and it was Cindy. I explained to her what I had told John and she was completely supportive. She held no judgment whatsoever. Immediately, she asked me to start giving her the list of items that I needed from my apartment and I began to rattle off my requests.

I explained where all my clothes were in the apartment. I told her I needed enough to get me through four days. In addition, I requested that she bring my journal and my Soduko book. I couldn't live without Soduko. It was the only way to get my mind off everything.

Then she asked if she could tell Stacy. I quickly agreed, knowing full well that if anyone would understand and not be judgmental, it was Stacy. She promised that either she or Stacy would come to the psychiatric ward that night to drop off my belongings. I was actually looking forward to seeing a familiar face, even under these intense circumstances.

Now it was a waiting game. It felt like I had been in the ER for days. I tried falling back asleep, but my body was just not into it. As I lay there, staring up at the ceiling, I began to formulate all of the to-dos that were waiting for me at work. Who was going to finish all of those items while I was out? No one else knew how to do them or even that they were due. Without a second thought, I called John again to schedule a conference call.

"Are you serious?" he asked. "Stop worrying so much about work and just focus on getting better. Things will be handled here."

I quickly replied with a sigh, "John, I can't relax until I know that these things are taken care of. Will you please humor me and call me tomorrow morning so I can walk you through the items that need to get completed? Please, just humor me."

He paused and then reluctantly agreed.

It was after five p.m. when a nurse finally came to escort me to the pysch ward. Having the energy to actually walk down the hospital corridors made me ecstatic. The only place I had walked that day was from my hospital bed to the bathroom.

Upon entering the psych ward, another nurse greeted me and asked me all sorts of familiar questions. I gave my brief history, once again, and the reasons why I thought I was being admitted. I summarized it all in about fifteen minutes—everything from the starving, the bingeing, the cutting, and the overdosing. Boy, was my life a train wreck. And, at that point, it didn't seem like there was any end in sight.

Shortly after my initial interview, I was given the tour. The unit was fairly small. The nurse first showed me my locker, where I was to keep all of my makeup, hairspray, and other beauty products. We were not allowed to keep any of these substances in our rooms. Additionally, she mentioned that we were not allowed to have any sharp objects on the floor at any time, including razors or scissors. If we had brought them to the unit, they would be kept behind the front desk until the day we were discharged. This meant no shaving for a few days. I felt like I was on an episode of Survivor.

Other banned items included pens, pencils, or any type of string, including shoelaces. Anything that residents could use to hurt themselves or to commit suicide was taken away. Luckily I was able to request a dull pencil for Sudoku. Thank God. I really don't know what I would have done without a writing utensil.

We then continued down the long corridor to the bedrooms. The unit somewhat reminded me of the EDU at Somerset Medical Center. The walls were neutral, while the carpeting covering the floor was a dark contrasting navy blue. Our rooms provided only the essentials: beds with army green blankets, one nightstand, and a dresser.

Toiletries in the bathroom were also basic, complete with conditioning shampoo—which doubled as our body soap, mind you—and a small tube of toothpaste. I had to put in a special request for a toothbrush and a comb that both appeared to have come from the dollar store. I paused for a moment and thought, "Really? And some people think camping is roughing it."

We finally made our way down to the common area, which consisted of a few group therapy rooms and a patient lounge. The group therapy rooms contained nothing more than chairs, positioned neatly in a circle. The patient lounge, however, contained some couches, tables and chairs for when we were dining, and a big-screen TV.

A large outdated VHS collection surrounded the TV, including movies such as *Hitch* and *Pretty Woman*. Just what I needed. Romantic comedies weren't exactly at the top of my list at the moment. At least I would have my Sudoku book and my journal. Those would be my sole sources of entertainment over the next few days.

Dinner was just being served as I entered the lounge.

"Let me see if they can send up another dinner for you," the nurse stated. "I'll be right back."

And with that, she left me there, standing in a room full of patients, none of whom knew me nor were making an attempt to, so I immediately wandered over to the couch positioned directly in front of the TV and took a seat. But sure enough, within minutes, the nurse was back with a dinner tray for me.

"This should be interesting," I thought to myself. Included on the tray next to the silver-domed entrée were paper menus for the following day. This would be my first hospital stay where I actually looked forward to choosing my meals. Eating was now a highlight, given the circumstances.

I opened up the dome to find a large slice of lasagna, coupled with some steamed broccoli on the side. I ate a few bites and decided right then to order cereal for the next day's meals. Yes, I ordered cereal for breakfast, lunch and dinner. Cereal was safe.

After I finished dinner, I went back over to the couch. I found it a bit odd that no one had taken the time to introduce themselves by this point. I guess everyone just kept to themselves. Well, everyone except Joe.

Joe was the man from the ER who had been singing the Grease tunes. Turns out he was next in line behind me to be admitted into the behavioral health unit. He turned up in the lounge close to when we were all finishing our meals.

As he sat down, he turned towards one of the nurses and loudly stated, "I like your hair. I've always liked short hair. Have you ever been a go-go dancer?"

Wow, this was going to be interesting, I thought to myself.

About an hour later, Cindy and Stacy arrived with my clothes; however, they were a few minutes past the end of visiting hours. Luckily, they were still able to drop off my stuff, but I wasn't allowed to see them. What a bummer. I was really looking forward to getting a hug. At least now I had my Sodoku book. That was going to be my saving grace.

I also received my journal, which gave me the ability to write about my thoughts and experiences. Writing was such great therapy at times like this. I wanted to record my feelings while I was there in order to figure out how I had gotten to this point and what I needed to do to fix it.

Before I went to bed, I decided to call my mom and dad. I knew deep down that I couldn't get through this without them. They needed to know so they could reach out and support me. So I did call, and I was glad that I did. They were both very understanding and both drove up to CT to be by my side.

Diary Entry: 2/20/2007

My roommate likes to talk. She's a small frail older woman, probably around forty-five or fifty years in age. She told me that she is a psychic. Tells lots of stories—can't figure out how many kids she has. Says her ex molested them and they all got taken away from her. Keeps telling me I should have babies, like a Jesus baby.

At 10:36 a.m., Joe fell asleep in group and started snoring. And he constantly farts in the main lounge. At 12:34 p.m., Mike, another male patient, probably around the age of twenty, tells me that a Liger can fly. As far as I knew, a Liger was a cross between a tiger and a lion and did not have wings. Of course, this was only based on my knowledge of the subject from what they discussed in the movie

Napolean Dynamite. *Mike had never even heard of* Napolean Dynamite. *Interesting.*

Stacy and John came to visit today. And I got lots of phone calls. My roommate put apple seeds in water and thinks they will grow into a tree overnight. Again, interesting.

10:15 p.m.—I go to my room and it smells like smoke. My roommate had brought in cigarettes, which were not allowed. They searched her stuff to find them. She tried blaming it on me, but alas, I've never smoked in my life so that wasn't a very believable tale. She also told me that she came in to the hospital to hide out. Apparently, she is needed in court to testify for a murder trial but she doesn't want to have any part in it. This day keeps getting better and better. And I feel so much more sane.

Diary Entry: 2/21/2007

Today, I woke up to a nurse asking to draw my blood which, let me tell you, is a very uneasy experience. And my roommate told me that I sleep beautifully—I shouldn't worry when I get married. She also complemented my sunset watercolor that I did in art class. I gave it to her. She thinks the pink in the sky represents love. "I will definitely find love one day, no worries," she says.

After my shower, an older woman, probably in her sixties, came into our room. Apparently, she told my roommate that she was worried that they were going to try to give her an abortion. My roommate told her not to worry. They only give them to people under two years old. What the hell was going on? I was really starting to feel normal.

8:34 a.m.—My roommate tells Mike a story. Starts out by saying her ex-husband abused her, but she still loves him so much. And I overheard someone else in the lounge just say it was December 25th. It was all so fascinating. I couldn't wait to get out.

Needless to say, there was continuous entertainment from the others in the unit. But aside from listening to their antics and interesting dialogue, most of my time was spent reflecting on my past and planning the immediate future. Things were going to have to change.

God had given me another chance to make things right. It was obviously not my time to go just yet, and I was going to have to work harder and smarter to make it through the pain. I was going to have to cut down on the workload so I didn't feel so overwhelmed, and I was going to have to succumb to the fact that I couldn't control everything, including the sale of my house and finalizing the divorce. Certain things were just going to take time, and I would have to learn patience. It was going to be hard, but I knew I could do it. At this point, I felt like I could get through anything.

On the day before I left the hospital, I made a list of things to remember. Ways to deal with issues or just life in general. They all seemed like common sense when I really took the time to think about each one, but I think everyone forgets every now and again what life is really all about.

We can get too caught up in the day-to-day minutia and the "what's next" and not enough time celebrating our accomplishments. I've found, over my years of therapy and reflection on life in general, that everyone needs to stop and smell the roses more often than they think.

Diary Entry: 2/21/2007

1. LEAN ON PEOPLE. *Get over the feeling of being a burden. You have many friends and family members that care about you. You would be there for them. Let them be there for you.*
2. LEARN HOW TO SAY NO. *You can't do everything. Prioritize and plan time accordingly. Leave enough time to relax and unwind, and don't forget to set realistic goals.*
3. CONTROL WHAT YOU CAN. *You know the serenity prayer inside and out. God, grant me the ability to accept the things I cannot change, the courage to change the things that I can, and the wisdom to know the difference. Enough said.*

4. EAT HEALTHY AND EXERCISE. *This will give you the energy to do everything you want to do.*
5. USE HEALTHY WAYS TO COPE WITH TOUGH SITUATIONS. *Call a friend. Do Sudoku. Write in your journal. Color. Whatever you need to do to take your mind off of the issue at hand.*
6. REWARD POSITIVE BEHAVIOR. *Celebrate the little things.*
7. THINK PEACEFUL THOUGHTS. *Beach, ocean, flowers, outlet shopping. Whatever brings a smile to your face.*
8. REMEMBER, LIFE IS GOOD. *What you get out of it depends on what you put in.*

This is your life, are you who you want to be
This is your life, is it everything you dreamed that it would be
When the world was younger and you had everything to lose

–Switchfoot, "This is Your Life"

9 | on a positive note

It's been three and a half years since I was discharged from the hospital, and I've accomplished everything that I had set out to do. My house was finally sold and the divorce became final, both within a few months after my hospitalization. From there, I focused my energy on finding a career path about which I could be passionate.

Through career counseling and networking, I not only figured out the position that I wanted but I also found a new job in the field. I moved into a new apartment complex, more convenient to work and social events. And although my financial situation isn't where I'd like it to be, I'm surviving just fine. I have my health and good friends on whom I can lean. My family isn't perfect, but they love me unconditionally, which is a luxury that should not be taken for granted. My hair isn't as thick as it used to be and I have a big butt. That's never going to change, and I think I'm okay with that. It's taken me thirty years to realize that life isn't perfect, but it is good. And I'm glad that I'm still living it.

Oh, why be perfect
No, it's not worth it
Don't be so obsessed–c'mon give it a rest
This is not some contest–just do your best
'Cause nobody's perfect

–Shania Twain, "What a way to wanna be"

quotables

Below is a collection of some of my favorite quotes and sayings that I've heard through the years. Each and every one of these has made me stop and think about life when I'm having a bad day.

"When we can begin to take our failures non-seriously, it means we are ceasing to be afraid of them. It is of immense importance to learn to laugh at ourselves."

–Katherine Mansfield

"Don't be fooled by me. Don't be fooled by the mask I wear…I give the impression that I'm secure, that all is sunny…but don't believe it…beneath dwells the real me, in confusion, in fear, in loneliness…I tell you everything that's really nothing, nothing of what's crying within me…don't be fooled by what I'm saying. Please listen carefully and try to hear what I'm not saying, what I'd like to be able to say, what—for survival—I need to say, but I can't say."

–Anonymous

"A woman is often measured by the things she cannot control. She is measured by the way her body curves or doesn't curve, by where she is flat, straight, or round. She is measured by 36-24-36 and inches and ages and numbers, by all outside things that don't ever add up to who she is on the inside. And so, if a woman is to be measured, let her be measured by the things she can control, by who she is and who she is trying to become..."

–Anonymous

CPSIA information can be obtained at www.ICGtesting.com
Printed in the USA
BVOW021847120412
287571BV00001B/38/P

9 781936 400591